Making Innovation Pay

People Who Turn IP into Shareholder Value

Making Innovation Pay

People Who Turn IP into Shareholder Value

EDITED BY BRUCE BERMAN

WILEY

John Wiley & Sons, Inc.

Published by John Wiley & Sons, Inc., Hoboken, New Jersey
Published simultaneously in Canada

For general information on our other products and services, or technical support, please contact our Customer Care Department within the United States at 800-762-2974, from outside the United States at 317-572-3993, or fax 317-572-4002.

Wiley also publishes its books in a variety of electronic formats. Some content that appears in print may not be available in electronic books.

For more information about Wiley products, visit our Web site at http://www.wiley.com.

Library of Congress Cataloging-in-Publication Data

Making innovation pay : people who turn IP into shareholder value / edited by Bruce Berman.

p.   cm.

Includes index.

ISBN-13: 978-0-471-73337-9 (cloth : alk. paper)

ISBN-10: 0-471-73337-7 (cloth : alk. paper)

1. Technological innovations —Economic aspects.   2. Patent licenses.

I. Berman, Bruce M.

HC79.T4M32   2006

658.4'063— dc22

2005031934

Printed in the United States of America

10 9 8 7 6 5 4 3 2

For spirited inventors, investors, and strategists whose imagination and perseverance expand the horizon.

About the Author

Bruce Berman is president of Brody Berman Associates, Inc. in New York, a management consulting and communications firm that works closely with innovation-based businesses, investors, and assets. The firm's areas of industry focus include information technology, science, law, and finance.

Bruce conceived and edited *From Ideas to Assets: Investing Wisely in Intellectual Property* (John Wiley & Sons, 2002), a widely acclaimed exploration of the business of IP that has been translated into Japanese. He has implemented public relations, investor relations, marketing, and business development programs on behalf of more than 200 businesses, and has counseled many executives, investors, and attorneys.

Bruce is a member of the editorial advisory boards of *Intellectual Asset Management* and *Patent Strategy & Management*. His column, *IP Investor*, appears regularly in London-based *IAM*. Articles, chapters, and reviews written by him have appeared in many periodicals and books, including *The Book of Investing Rules* (Financial Times, Prentice-Hall, 2003), which *The Motley Fool* called one of the ten most useful investment books. He has been cited as a resource in many business, technology, and IP publications. A previous book which he also edited and contributed to, *Hidden Value: Profiting from the Intellectual Property Economy* (Euromoney Institutional Investor), was published in London in 1999.

A frequent speaker, Bruce has guest lectured at Columbia University School of Business and either chaired conferences or moderated panels for The Wall Street Transcript IP conference on ROI, the Intellectual Property Owners' Association "patent trolls" conference in Washington, D.C., and the 2005 Center for Intellectual Property Studies conference in Gothenberg, Sweden.

Bruce received his Master's degree in film scholarship from Columbia University, where he taught for three years and also completed course and comprehensive requirements for his Ph.D. He received his Bachelor of Arts degree with honors in English literature and journalism from The City College of New York. Bruce lives with his wife and daughter in Westchester County, NY.

Contents

Acknowledgments

Incorporating the ideas of leading innovators into a single book is more difficult than it may appear. I am indebted to all those, named and not, who played a part in the preparation of *Making Innovation Pay*. Some were vital to the research, others with securing contributors and fleshing out my thinking, and still others with organization, content, and design.

Among those whose ideas and feedback helped pave the way for this book were Keith Bergelt, Wendy Chou, Mike Dunn, Harry Gwinnell, Bo Heiden, Tomas Kellner, Ron Laurie, Sam Mamudi, Marius Meland, Ulf Petrusson, Andrew Riddles, Robert Shepard, Herb Wamsley, David Wanetick, Joff Wild, and Jim Woods. It also is necessary to mention the many IP directors, licensing executives, IP lawyers, and bankers who unselfishly availed me of their knowledge, time, and experience. Special thanks to Brenda Pomerance, my gracious business partner and patent attorney.

The help of my humble assistants Shirley Wang, Angelina Lachhman, and Anuja Gagoomal with proofing the manuscript and in preparing many of the charts and tables cannot go unheralded. A hearty thank you to my Wiley editor Susan McDermott, who had the confidence to let me have my way (some of the time) and the constitution to endure our second collaboration. Thanks also to my loyal production editor, Natasha Wolfe, and the entire Wiley team.

A special debt of gratitude to my family, Sharon, Jenn, and Tucker, for putting up with my limited focus during MIP's gestation and birthing.

Finally, I am profoundly grateful to each contributor to this book for their trust, patience, and for rising to my challenges and offering me theirs.

Foreword

So, you've picked up *Making Innovation Pay,* and you're trying to understand why you should be spending your time (and money) learning about patents. You might be thinking there are already enough books on this topic to rebuild New Orleans' beleaguered levees—and you may be right. Innovation touches everyone.

But this book is different.

In *Making Innovation Pay,* Bruce Berman has persuaded, arm-twisted, and otherwise cajoled today's most successful patent practitioners into telling their stories and allowing him to tell theirs. Until now, no book has discussed innovation in so resolutely clear-eyed, personal, and practical business terms. Bruce Berman's previous book, *From Ideas to Assets,* was a tantalizing and thorough overview of IP possibilities. *Making Innovation Pay* zeros in on the successes and the people behind them.

Nowhere else will you find Ron Katz, one of the most successful inventors in history, reflecting on the "trade secrets" of licensing. Two of today's great IP litigators, Ron Schutz and Ray Niro, define what it takes to win patent cases and who benefits from them. Corporate IP officers abound in this book, including Marshall Phelps (chief IP strategist at Microsoft and former head at IBM), Joe Beyers (Marshall's counterpart at Hewlett Packard), Peter Detkin (IP investor and former Intel patent chief who coined the term patent "troll"), Dan McCurdy (ThinkFire CEO and former president of IP business at Lucent and a key player at IBM Research), and Jim Malackowski (the heavy hitter running the IP investment bank Ocean-Tomo, who persuaded billionaire Ross Perot to put almost $200 million into an IP capital fund).

Contributors explain the illusion of patent exclusivity and how best to regard invention rights, realistically, from the perspective of corporate profit and business advantage. Not to be outdone, Alex Poltorak, an accomplished physicist and purveyor of IP assets, addresses the controversial patent "troll" issue with a bit of tongue in cheek. As if these insights were not enough, Bruce Lehman (longest serving USPTO Commissioner) steps up to help us understand the worldwide impact wrought by the influx of uncertain patents and costly disputes.

This book breaks new ground by giving voice to resourceful and articulate individuals who have had the courage to brave new trails and the generosity to share how they do it. Bruce's own provocative opening chapter, "Roadblocks or Building Blocks?," sets the tone.

Innovation and patents are transforming the world. With globalization, outsourcing, and offshoring, the world is getting smaller and, as a competitive playing field, flatter. Most companies no longer own all of their means of manufacturing or distribution. Securing and managing intellectual property rights have emerged from a back-office legal function to the foundation of corporate strategy. Today, ideas— and the right to use them—are as much products as microprocessors and cell phones. To compete, businesses require a centralized IP strategy that facilitates competitive returns and enhances shareholder value.

IP management needs novel and more collaborative business models. Companies and independent inventors alike must learn when and with whom it may be beneficial for them to share IP rights, and how these good deeds may also be wise business practices. Relying solely on the exclusionary approaches of the past no longer works. Business questions need answering: When is it beneficial to a company to help a community with IP donations, and how is this best accomplished? How can organizations shape IP policies to create innovation networks for their advantage? Without new IP thinking, how can companies go "open" in some parts of the value chain, while creating sustainable shareholder value in others? How can the world's IP regimes be harmonized to help global trade? How can the patent offices ensure that society benefits from the highest quality protection? But these are questions for another book.

Since the publication of my book *Rembrandts in the Attic* in 1999, I am frequently called on to speak to senior managements and boards about assessing IP results. *Making Innovation Pay* is essential reading for anyone interested in technology, performance, or value. It is also useful for getting a handle on a new worldview.

Would I buy a copy of this book had I not contributed the foreword? I'd buy two. One for me, and one for a good friend. Many thanks to Bruce Berman for providing it.

KEVIN G. RIVETTE
Vice President,
Intellectual Property Strategy
IBM Corporation

Introduction

If business is a high wire act, then the business of innovation is like being shot out of a cannon, blindfolded.

Everyone says innovation is important, but almost no one agrees on the best way to profit from it. My inspiration for *Making Innovation Pay* is to examine the relationship between ideas, capital, and strong leadership. Exploring how technology rights become shareholder value is a pursuit whose time has come.

This book looks at the techniques for achieving the best return on inventions and provides a glimpse at the people who deploy them. The ten contributors are all on the leading edge of an emerging industry. They comprise a veritable pantheon of IP talent, who, I sincerely believe, are making history as they write about it. They are mavericks, perhaps not universally admired by their adversaries or recognized by Wall Street, but quintessentially American in their desire to succeed where none have before them.

In most cases they have amassed significant fortunes for their employers, clients, and themselves. Readers interested in science, technology, finance, investment returns, or the art of the deal should find this book especially enlightening.

Senior managements have been woefully ignorant about how to identify and use IP assets to enhance shareholder value. Those who have been successful with IP often do so despite traditional leadership, not because of it. Some are changing because they want to, others because they must.

I have been looking at IP from a business perspective for more than a decade. My previous books, *Hidden Value* (1999) and *From Ideas to Assets* (2002), attempted to make IP strategy more meaningful to a broader audience. *Making Innovation Pay* cuts to the chase. It addresses the questions "Who is making money from IP rights?" and "How are they doing it?" It also probes what equips some individuals to generate higher IP-related profits than others.

It took considerable coaxing to get leading IP asset managers to talk openly about their experiences. A closed-mouthed group, they normally prefer to fly under the radar. The result, I believe, is candid perspectives by and about ten guiding IP lights regarding the role rights play in enhancing results. Readers who seek from this book a foundation for discussion and debate will not be disappointed.

The Earliest Innovators

It is no accident that the Founding Fathers embraced invention and IP exclusivity. Franklin was a renowned inventor; Jefferson was an inventor and designer, as well as the first Commissioner of Patents. But it took the astute market sense of Madison and Hamilton, as well as patentee Lincoln, to understand how competitive forces and innovation can shape prosperity.

I have had the privilege to get to know all of the contributors and have worked closely with some of them. In most cases they are atypical, strong-minded individualists who avoid easy definition. Until recently, patents—the exclusive rights that protect inventions—have been used primarily as a defensive shield. The focus was on freedom to operate and keeping others out of the market. But today people are finding new, more effective ways for using patents to maximize shareholder value. Some of these methods are counterintuitive; others are downright unpleasant; often, as in the case of patent "trolls," their complexity can cause folklore to be confused with fact.

The people who make innovation pay are pioneers. They include forward-thinking engineers and scientists, financial analysts, and lawyers, managers and investors. They excel at synthesizing diverse disciplines and discerning complex markets, and they revel in the art of negotiation. Intellectual property and intangible assets today comprise 80% of the market value of the S&P 500, yet most CFOs spend barely 20% of their time managing them. Invention rights have emerged as a valuable new form of currency and, not coincidentally, a key to the future. I hope that *Making Innovation Pay* opens the door.

BRUCE BERMAN
New York City
January 2006

In the world's history, certain inventions and discoveries occurred, of peculiar value, on account of their great efficiency in facilitating all other inventions and discoveries. Of these were the arts of writing and of printing, the discovery of America, and the introduction of Patent-laws.

—Abraham Lincoln, 1859

Roadblocks or Building Blocks?

BY BRUCE BERMAN

Most companies are reluctant to get the best return on their most valuable assets. Shareholder value be damned. Fear of provoking costly lawsuits plays a part. So does confusion about what intellectual property is and how best to deploy it. Being publicly branded a patent "troll" adds to the turmoil.

Patent trolls are controversial not because of the destruction attributed to them, but because they strike at the heart of the complex relationship between innovation and commerce. The term has become synonymous with the unfair assertion of IP rights and extortion of damage payments. An Intel Corp. lawyer came up with the name in 2001 in response to a rash of attacks on the company's inventions, apparently from financial speculators who acquired random patents from failed companies and independent inventors that related to Intel products.

The author wishes to thank *IAM* magazine for allowing him to use its pages to develop these and other ideas, which are not necessarily the opinion of Brody Berman Associates.

FIGURE 1.1

Source: Kim Hart/Roger Harding Picture Library

Trolling for Dollars. "It's going to cost you to invalidate my patent," nuisance asserters say. "Pay a law firm to defend your company and waste time and money, or pay me less to go away."

These asserters were not in the business of manufacturing microprocessors or semi-conductors, but in recovering damages and collecting royalties on the unauthorized use of their rights—kind of a "gotcha" business. But despite Intel's legitimate pain, there is a distinct difference between those gaming the system in search of a quick buck and those legitimate purveyors of patent value who are able to acquire cheaply or otherwise gain control of important patents that read on others' products intending to make a profit. To the defendant they may look the same. A true troll might ask hundreds of large companies for $50 million or more but accept a quick settlement for a few hundred thousand dollars, less than the cost of preliminary litigation, to disappear (Figure 1.1).

A patent is a negative right. It does not allow the owner to practice an invention but confers the privilege to defend it. Unfortunately, patentees cannot dial 911 for the local police and say "Arrest that man. He's stealing my invention." They need to bring an expensive, time-consuming suit, something small companies and independent inventors can seldom afford. The average patent suit costs $3.5 million, and many significant ones are $10 to $15 million. Some exceed $60 million. Litigation of this type has been called "the Sport of Kings." Today, it can cost a defendant $1 million to neutralize a single, glaringly weak patent, something even large companies find daunting.

WORTHY OPPONENTS

Those with bulging patent portfolios in the past relied on smaller companies and independent inventors to lack the resources or hubris to do battle. Today, they are finding them worthy opponents. In fact, an independent inventor's very lack of portfolio patents for a defendant to counterattack has become a new source of leverage. High costs, the increased uncertainty of issued patents, better competitive analysis, and broader interest by private investors in strategic rights have caused the tables to turn.

Astute investors have discovered how weaknesses inherent in the patent system regarding *pendency* (the time it takes a patent to issue) and *validity* (whether it should have been issued in the first place), coupled with inadequate intellectual property defenses, can be exploited for financial gain. They are aware of how vulnerable many large, risk-adverse companies are, and how, in most cases, it makes business sense for them to settle rather than take their chances before judges or juries. In the past, finding expert IP counsel to take a patent assertion was close to impossible. Law firms did not wish to support smaller entities against what could be current or future clients. Although it is still difficult to get a major IP law firm or practice to take on some patent assertion cases, well-funded independents today are finding it easier to get quality representation, especially if they pay their lawyers a percentage of what they recover. Indeed, the high cost and protracted length of patent disputes, coupled with the uncertainty of patents being issued today and the tendency of courts to uphold them, have set the stage for a patent crisis of global proportions. (Thirteen of the top 20 recipients of U.S. patents in 2004 were foreign-based companies.) The crisis affects everything from the high cost of research and development to the pace and quality of innovation, as well as shareholder value.

Eighty percent of the market value of S&P 500 companies is attributed to intangible assets, much of it patents and trademarks. With patent rights less certain and more frequently put to the test, even companies with well-built portfolios are vulnerable. But doing business in a market-based system means that all asset holders have equal right to maximum value, even if some have acquired a strategic advantage. Many companies are discovering that filing for and receiving a lot of patents is a less effective deterrent than it once was. The National Academy of Sciences is calling for more funding for the U.S. Patent and Trademark Office (USPTO), where 3,000 examiners handle some 350,000 applications annually, often with far too little time and experience to identify the all-relevant prior "art" to determine if an invention is truly original.

Anti-troll advocates say that examinations often result in many patents being granted that should not see the light of day. Studies show that half of all issued U.S. patents should not have been approved and that the USPTO green-lights more than 95% of all original patent applications. Patent examinations must improve. However, it is naïve to think that this change alone will solve all of the ills of an eternally overburdened, yet essentially reliable, patent system. Patent holders, regardless of size, financial commitment, or commercialization strategy, have the right to prevent unauthorized use of their inventions. Unfortunately, regarding patents as financial assets is a more difficult concept for some than others.

DISTINGUISHING PATENT TROLLS FROM INDEPENDENT ASSERTERS

Independent asserters is a more accurate term than trolls for those who choose to defend invention rights against infringers by entering into a licensing agreement or, if necessary, filing a lawsuit. This is more than semantics. Thoughtful IP owners are advised to refrain from applying labels that could be used to denigrate their own best practices. There is no prohibition against acquiring, owning, or enforcing patent rights without practicing them, or in deploying intangible assets wisely. It is no crime for patentees to expose weaknesses and ask for reasonable royalties, if they can prove their rights are being infringed. The paradigm shift reflected in how IP rights are identified and deployed may be frustrating for some, but it is surely here to stay. Profiting from innovation and providing value to shareholders may require that portfolio owners think more like their attackers. Innovative IP management strategies help make innovation pay.

Some companies may be taking a page from the independents' handbook. *Newsweek* and other sources report that Sony, Intel, Nokia, and Microsoft, among others, have invested anywhere from $350 to $600 million in a patent acquisition fund. Google and eBay also are part of the group. What the fund plans to do with these patents is unclear, but a significant investment return is expected. Other companies with large IP portfolios are even segregating their assets by placing them into a special-purpose entity (SPE) remote from easy counterassertion.

Innovation is the developed world's greatest asset. Although companies need more reliable, better-researched, and timelier patents, they also need more efficient mechanisms for resolving disputes. Perhaps the greatest threat to return on innovation (I call it, ROIP) is the one-two punch of uncertainty and cost. Defendants have a good point. It should not require a million dollars nor take two or more years to prove that a dubious patent is invalid. Patent disputes are inevitable. How they get resolved is not.

Many of the large patentees that protest loudest ultimately rely on USPTO inefficiencies to build, defend, and profit from their inventions. It would be terrific if the USPTO (and the European Patent Office and Japan Patent Office) harmonized to issue more reliable patents that could not be so readily, and expensively, invalidated. (The rate is about one in three.) But because of high costs and difficulty retaining experienced examiners (who often go to work for law firms), that change is not likely to occur any time soon. Traditional patent litigation may not be the solution, but neither are unrealistic expectations about improving examination standards or paying lip service to patent quality.

Companies started the IP wars in the 1980s with significant resources — large patent portfolios and huge litigation war chests and the patience to dig in for the long haul. At that time, few inventors and businesses had sufficient means to defend themselves. There was little for most active filers to fear. Today, well-informed and well-funded patent owners, and even law firms, are prepared to challenge complex invention rights. The takeaway: large patent portfolios do not necessarily consist of relevant or reliable patents, and, as a result, some companies are vulnerable.

Like nuclear powers, patentees with significant portfolios are armed to defend themselves primarily against their world-class peers. Mutually assured destruction is reason enough not to deploy all of the weapons in their arsenals. Many disputes are settled with gentlemanly cross-licenses. However, in a guerrilla war—the kind independent owners are likely to wage—Goliaths are often more vulnerable than Davids.

Companies do themselves a disservice by whining about the unfairness of the patent system, which they may have helped perpetuate. Until now, many have talked about the need for patent quality but have done little, or, at least, not enough, to facilitate it. It is time for truly innovative companies to step up. Stronger, better-researched patents, smarter enforcement strategies, and more prudent approaches to licensing and dispute resolution and IP asset monetization should be the rule, not the exception. Most patentees agree that granting exclusive rights on truly new inventions and features, and establishing their value as intangible assets, has a generally positive long-term effect on innovation and shareholder value. Companies' reluctance to manage their IP proactively, for fear that doing so might be seen as unethical or peripheral to their core business, need to be introduced to the 21st century. They also need to be less arrogant about the ubiquity of their portfolios, despite their bulk or cost. The fact is, some companies' patents are more questionable and short lived than they are willing to admit. Smart investors are in a better position than ever to prove it.

High-Stakes Poker

Determining where patent extortion ends and responsible IP management begins is a question that should keep management up at night, but it's probably not even on their radar screen. Few CEOs are asking questions like, "How do we know we are getting a proper return on our IP?" or "Have we reserved sufficiently for possible infringement assertions in our industry, legitimate or otherwise?" Corporate officers and directors have a legal and moral obligation to manage all company assets for maximum shareholder value. This means acting strategically to exact maximum return on intangibles like innovation and patent rights. How many are at least considering deploying patent rights for ROI and not for market share? Not too many. *IP Frontline* estimates that at IP-rich Cisco in 2004, for example, the CFO was spending approximately 90% of his time on just 25% of the company's market value. I would wager that most CFOs spend little of their precious time managing their company's most important assets. This is in part because tangibles like real estate and inventory are much easier to deal with under GAAP than intangibles like IP rights which, for accounting purposes, still are swept into "goodwill." The somewhat puritanical notion that there are more acceptable and unacceptable ways of making innovation pay speaks more to a lack of understanding of IP market dynamics than to higher ethics. In the early 1990s, Texas Instruments busted open this myth with a series of aggressive and lucrative patent assertions.

More dangerous than trolls is the notion that it is wrong to use IP such as patents and know-how (trade secrets) and knowledge of the patent system for financial gain. Companies employ tax strategies to the benefit of shareholders, so why not patent strategies? It's difficult to condone the deployment of patents that should never have been issued in the first place or are taking too long to issue. However, they exist in every patentee's portfolio, and various levels of dispute resolution (costly as they may be) exist to sort things out. It is not a crime to buy low and sell higher.

Patent enforcement is a high-stakes poker game. Sometimes it costs money to call a bluff; generally, the better bank-rolled survive, but not always. The inequities of the patent office are applied fairly democratically. Patent reform is not an easy fix. Vested interests divide even companies within the same industry, let alone independent inventors and R&D behemoths. Large portfolio owners use the system against competitors small and large, and so, too, do independent patent owners, who don't practice them, use the system against defendants. No matter how they are acquired, enforced, or otherwise monetized, the same rights exist for all patent owners, regardless of their business strategy or capital investment. Some patentees, however, are better prepared to profit from companies' weaknesses than others. Similar to First Amendment and free-trade rights, it is potentially dangerous to apply patent protections selectively because defendants appear to have more at stake. Assuring primary and secondary IP owners their due, while painful for some, typically leads to higher asset values for all.

Some independent owners purchase rights from down-on-their-luck inventors who cannot afford to enforce their rights; others share with inventors in the potential recoveries. Most are willing to put their money where their accusations are. This newfound perseverance scares the heck out of companies that are not used to having their freedom to operate challenged by a relative small fry.

The upswing in patent suits (152% over a recent 12-year period) and reluctance to go to trial (Figure 1.2) because of cost and uncertainty illustrates that, despite the R&D dollars and legal investment that underlie many IP portfolios, they afford less protection than they appear to provide. Companies' desire to minimize risk has grown. Demonizing all patent asserters adds to the confusion. It makes it more difficult for CEOs, board members, and others to distinguish between shakedown artists out for a quick buck from those that can inflict lasting damage. The business media, which is ill-informed, fans the flames of these misunderstandings. Consider the following example.

A Double Standard for IP Assets

Donald Trump is planning his next Manhattan skyscraper. He has acquired a suitable site on First Avenue, near the United Nations. A small parking lot, 20 feet wide, blocks access to part of the proposed building's lobby. The newly signed lease on the lot does not expire until 2011. If Trump wishes to build his luxury tower soon, he will have to purchase the land and acquire the lease at a hefty premium to the market.

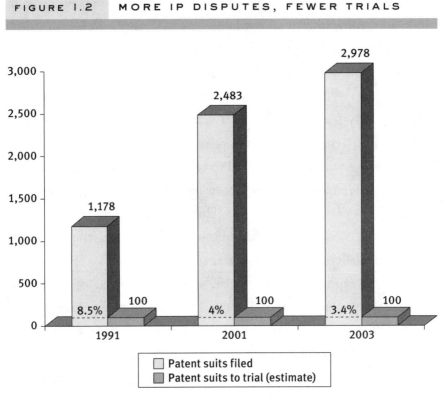

FIGURE 1.2   MORE IP DISPUTES, FEWER TRIALS

Patent suits filed
Patent suits to trial (estimate)

Source: © Brody Berman Associates, Inc.

Patent suits are up 152% over a 12 year period between 1991 and 2003. Over the same period, the number of costly trials is virtually flat at about 100. As a percentage of suits filed, patent trials are actually going down. The risk of having to pay damages, general uncertainty about the outcome of disputes, and legal fees have been blamed for the settlement trend.

In this example, the astute parking lot owner is likely to be viewed as a smart businessman, a capitalist, who through vision, luck, or both has beaten The Donald at his own game. This person is not preventing progress; he is merely making it a little more expensive for Trump, and possibly his tenants, who are prospective luxury condominium owners. Such is the cost of doing business in New York City. However, if an individual or company controlled a strategic intangible asset, such as a patent, that blocked an optical switching system from being sold or the introduction of a generic drug, the cry would likely be "unfair competition."

Patent exploiters who do not manufacture or practice what they invent tend to be seen as those who impede progress. They are painted as extortionists, or worse. Real estate speculators, however, no matter how ruthless or profitable, are seen as merely shrewd investors. A double standard exists when it comes to generating a return on intellectual assets, especially patent rights. Large portfolio holders must be careful what they wish for. Discouraging the market from determining value can be costly over the long haul. IP stakeholders take note.

Part of the problem is that IP assets are not easily defined. A combination of innovation, market demand, and legal rights, patents are highly complex, and their role in most products is not readily apparent. Rights violations are difficult to identify, expensive to document, and arduous to litigate. Although valuable patents are deserving of the recognition, when it comes to enforcing them, they are rarely afforded the same level of respect as worthwhile hard assets, such as real estate or natural resources. Compounding the problem is the proliferation of and access to digital content, such as music, movies, and books. Most law-abiding citizens believe that because good copies of digital content are easily made, they are there for the taking. If a teenager leaves a Virgin Megastore with the latest 50 Cent CD in his pocket and no sales receipt, he is shoplifting. If he downloads the same content from the Internet or a friend's CD and burns onto his PC or uploads into his iPod, he is exercising his rights under freedom of expression. Right.

It's amazing how many intelligent investors (Ben Graham, forgive me) and sophisticated, well-meaning executives still have difficulty taking intangibles seriously. To be fair, valuing IP is not an easy task. Even describing it can be a challenge. Unlike the equity, bond, or real estate markets, most patents are illiquid, and transactions are seldom transparent. A common vocabulary for describing IP assets, strongly suggested by the U.S. Securities and Exchange Commission (SEC) and the Licensing Executives Society, has yet to be adopted. New Financial Accounting Standards Board (FASB) accounting regulation established in 2001 require intangible assets included in an acquisition, such as IP, to be valued and written down within one year if they fail to meet certain impairment tests. No longer can companies dump intangibles into goodwill or allow them to languish for 20 years or more as part of an expensing schedule. This is a good start, but no cigar.

The term of limited exclusivity (that ends 20 years from filing in the United States) conferred on patents by the various governments in return for disclosing the details of an invention is designed to foster innovation, not impede it. In general, the U.S. patent system has done an exceedingly good job at achieving this goal. Disputes are the inevitable by-product of more rights and greater complexity, especially in a knowledge-centric economy that places a high premium on valuable ideas. An orderly, less contentious market for exchanging IP rights not only facilitates demand, but it encourages more accurate pricing and fuels investment in innovation. Unfortunately, it is easier discussed than established.

Tolls, Trolls, and U-Turns

Few patents, no more than 3% to 5% by most accounts, have significant value. Even worse, not many people are clear about what gives the valuable ones their importance. Speculating on IP rights is not very different from investing in real property. The difference is that a ready market for commercial or residential properties helps establish price stability and generate demand. Most people get it when it comes to bricks and mortar, but few do when it comes to prime IP assets. Taking a financial position in an intangible asset, whether the owner plans to commercialize or otherwise exploit it, should not be viewed as an unnatural act.

Several years ago an inventor decided to license key telecom patents he once had owned and practiced. His tiny company has generated more than $1 billion, almost all of it profit, through 2005 because he has enforced patents he owns that others require to do business. But a toll road is not necessarily a "troll" road (It certainly is not a one-way street.). Although the toll road presented by royalty payments may have cost some companies and consumers in the short run, it also increased the value of new technologies and products, and created a stronger market for related patents. In all likelihood, it increased shareholder value for licensees by hundreds of millions of dollars.

Savvy IP entrepreneurs are no more responsible for impeding progress than were speculators who purchased land in Kansas in the 1860s in anticipation of the transcontinental railroad. Nobody likes to pay a toll if they don't have to, but riding on a smoother, straighter highway can save considerable time and money. For an innovation-based company, it can make a world of competitive difference. A traveler can try to find his or her own route, but it is often not worth it. The Kansas speculators were neither settlers nor railway owners, but businessmen who sought to buy land cheaply and then either lease it or resell it at a higher rate. At first, the railroad companies were indignant about having to pay a toll to complete their route. In the end, cooler heads prevailed, and the roadblocks became building blocks for wealth on the new frontier.

With regard to monopolies they are justly classed among the greatest nuisances in government. But is it clear that as encouragements to literary works and ingenious discoveries, they are not too valuable to be wholly renounced? . . . It is much more to be dreaded that the few will be unnecessarily sacrificed to the many.

—James Madison to Thomas Jefferson, 1788

Turning a Patent Portfolio into a Profit Center

BY MARSHALL PHELPS

Profile: Hail to the Chief IP Officer

"IBM had been losing market share and its return on patents was poor," recalls Marshall Phelps. It was 1991, and he had just been put in charge of IBM's fledgling licensing business, an assignment he had requested. After years of pleading his case before CEO John Opel to regard patent rights as a profit center, not just as legal overhead, the chief executive relented. "He finally told me to go away and do it. Just make sure it doesn't cost the company too much money."

Marshall Phelps has been running 35–40 miles per week for almost 40 years.

Not only did it not cost IBM money, but in a little over a decade, Phelps grew the IP licensing business at IBM into $1 billion plus in annual revenues on margins exceeding 90%.

It was Phelps's hunch that after the anti-trust consent decree that IBM was subject to, and after the establishment of the Court of Appeals for the Federal Circuit in 1982, IBM's patents had to be worth more. Phelps helped establish the company's dominance in the area not by suing people for damages, as Texas Instruments had in the early 1990s, but by establishing intricate cross-licenses and product sales tied to IBM rights. Also, he established a way to link patent licenses to trade secrets, or know-how ("show-how"), which was once thought to be corporate suicide.

Phelps, now 60, retired from IBM in 2000 to work as CEO for a division of Spencer Trask, specializing in spin-offs from major corporations, such as Motorola and Lockheed Martin. Nathan Myhrvold contacted him in 2002 to serve as co-chairman of ThinkFire Services, a unique patent licensing and management company headed by Dan McCurdy, who was previously president of IP business at Lucent. (McCurdy is a contributor to this book.) Phelps was working with Myhrvold, former Microsoft Chief Technology Officer and CEO of Intellectual Ventures (see IV Managing Director Peter Detkin's chapter on patent triage), when a call came from Bill Gates, who wanted Phelps to achieve for Microsoft what he did for IBM. "It took calls on three successive nights for me to say, 'Yes, I'll take the job.'"

Phelps's title at Microsoft is corporate vice president and deputy general counsel for intellectual property. In essence, he is the company's chief IP strategist and business generator. Like Kevin Rivette at IBM and Joe Beyers at HP, Phelps's newly emerged position, effectively, CIPO, reports on a dotted line to the CEO and board of directors. This gives IP newfound respect at the highest levels of the corporation. Since Phelps joined Microsoft, the company's patent filings are in the top five among all U.S. filers, and several key litigations have been either settled or dismissed. He oversees Microsoft's various IP groups and management of its IP portfolio, which comprises some 3,000 U.S.-issued patents, their foreign counterparts, and more than 11,000 trademark registrations worldwide.

His 28-year career at IBM Corp. included serving as VP for IP and licensing. He was instrumental in IBM's standards and telecom policy, industry relations, patent licensing program, and IP portfolio development. Phelps helped establish IBM's Asia Pacific headquarters in Tokyo, where he spent four years, and served as the company's director of government relations in Washington, D.C.

Phelps and his wife, Eileen, divide their time between Kirkland, Washington, and New Canaan, Connecticut. He had been driving a Porsche Carrera 4 Turbo, which he calls "a track racer without a fire extinguisher," but has since given it up for a Honda hybrid when in Washington.

He has been an avid runner for almost 40 years and still runs 35 to 40 miles per week. His secret to running longevity is to change running shoes every 90 days, even if they do not appear worn. He enjoys reading, usually fiction, and can be found in bookstores when he has a free moment on the road. He has read at least one book per week for 30 years. Phelps, who dabbles in California real estate, has two grown children, a son who is an M&A lawyer in Los Angeles and a daughter who worked in the fashion industry and currently is a stay-at-home mom.

He obtained a business degree from Stanford long before it was fashionable for lawyers to have one and attributes at least part of his success to business, not legal prowess, and to trusting his instincts. He sits on the board of the International Institute for Intellectual Property, an IP think tank and educational organization based in Washington, D.C.

"Nothing is more counterintuitive than giving possible competitors access to your inventions and know-how," says Phelps. "Most CEOs think you are crazy to license them."

In the following chapter, he discusses how he helped people like IBM CEO Lou Gerstner understand why licensing makes sense both for income and business development, and what managers need to know about IP to succeed.

For most companies, a patent licensing program is an afterthought. Patents are secured for defensive purposes and filed away, without a thought to the revenue these rights might generate. Given the unusually high profit margins associated with licensing the rights to inventions, patents should be among companies' top priorities. The shortsightedness is due in part to (1) the belief that generating revenue from patents is inappropriate—an act of "extortion," say some; (2) the perception that there are insufficient resources to mount a successful licensing program; and (3) fear of "giving away" rights that may someday, under certain circumstances, be valuable.

The point of an effective licensing program is for patent owners to receive far greater return from a business perspective than what they give up. Unfortunately, patent owners with significant portfolios often fail to see it this way. Perhaps it is because they have difficulty accessing what their IP resources mean and how they can be deployed to support company objectives.

For those managers who determine that monetizing a patent portfolio is appropriate, the most challenging aspect of setting up a program will be convincing senior management, and especially the CEO, that it makes business sense. Most companies do not have broad-based out-licensing programs because they are counterintuitive. Management is blinded by two false assumptions: (1) that patents effectively deter infringement, and (2) that licensing patents somehow undermines a company's competitive edge by removing barriers to competition. For most companies, nothing could be further from the truth.

In addition to huge R&D expenditures, companies often spend large sums identifying and utilizing appropriate protective regimes for intellectual assets. The cost of filing and getting a single patent to issue in the United States can be upward of $20,000. (Copyrighted and trademarked materials present some of the same issues.) Executives like to think of these secured rights as little "monopolies," which insulate them from direct competition. After taking their company through the R&D mill (for many companies, to the tune of several billion dollars annually), the expense and effort to obtain statutory legal status (tens of millions of dollars) in multiple worldwide jurisdictions, multiple times, why would any executive in his or her right mind license these intangible assets to anyone, let alone to one or more direct competitors? Isn't it crazy, even suicidal, to do that? Lou Gerstner raised just that issue upon joining IBM as its CEO in the early 1990s.

THINKPAD®: THE LICENSING STORY

Lou joined IBM fresh from Nabisco, which had long been engaged in a brutal struggle over soft chocolate chip cookie manufacturing. (Nabisco had to pay Procter & Gamble $125 million in damages.) He believed patents were a fine way to stop an erstwhile competitor in its tracks, but they were not good for much more. Alas, reality is often different from belief. Although patents do confer the right to prohibit others from practicing your invention, enforcement can be difficult, expensive, time consuming, and unpredictable. Moreover, as is often the case, you may discover you need others' IP assets to efficiently optimize your own business.

Such was the situation faced by IBM. The example — the IBM ThinkPad® laptop of its day. Because IBM created the architecture of the vast majority of PCs in use at the time, it was a fair presumption that IBM needed little IP from others to build and sell such machines. This assumption was incorrect, however. To prove the point, we pried the top off an IBM laptop and glued little red flags to components in the machine that IBM licensed from others. We ran out of room at around 150 flags, with more IP yet to be identified. Inventions owned by others and required in the ThinkPad encompassed key aspects of the most important elements in the machine: memory, hard drives, architectures, processors, and so on.

Lou immediately got the point that IBM's freedom to operate and its ability to profit from its own and others' products had a great deal to do with the strength of its patent position. The company's aggressive outlicensing program continued apace. (The ThinkPad did not represent a problem for IBM because the company was so broadly cross-licensed within the IT industry that it had plenty of freedom of action.) Here we had the convergence of two important effects of years of licensing and cross-licensing activities: (1) royalties received for the right to use IBM's IP, and (2) IBM's ability to appropriately use the inventions of others, each gained through the trading of IP portfolios (Figure 2.1).

When it comes to patent licensing, companies have many choices amid three general options:

1. **They can refuse to license, period.** This might be, and probably is, more appropriate when a particular patent and a product take on a one-to-one characteristic. Drugs and chemical formulations come to mind. In these industries, it is easier to identify a direct cause-and-effect relationship between an invention and the specific rights that cover it. However, even here, because of the extraordinary costs of development in those industries, IP is often exchanged in other ways, such as joint development programs with smaller companies and with research institutions, such as universities on the front end. As described previously, in the electronics or IT industries, this model does not usually work for very long.

2. **They may do nothing with their IP.** If you are a stakeholder in such a company, you might well wonder why, in such an instance, the company spends money protecting its IP assets at all.

FIGURE 2.1

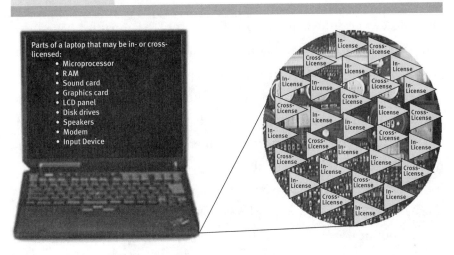

Parts of a laptop that may be in- or cross-licensed:
- Microprocessor
- RAM
- Sound card
- Graphics card
- LCD panel
- Disk drives
- Speakers
- Modem
- Input Device

Thinking about the ThinkPad®. Since IBM created the architecture for many of the PC's in use in the early 1990s, it seemed fair to assume it needed little IP help from others to build and sell these machines. Not true. CEO Louis Gerstner learned that more than 150 in- and cross-licenses gave IBM the freedom to operate and enhanced its ability to profit.

By doing nothing, the company could even find itself in a disadvantageous legal position going forward. In addition, if a company isn't even bothering to protect the fruits of its research and development by extracting market value or higher, you might well question your investment in the first place!

3. **They can leverage the company's portfolio in an appropriate fashion—by seeking a return on R&D.** In considering a licensing program, all companies are different, and different companies have differences within themselves. It is not unusual for a well-thought-out company program to consist of "programs" with aspects of all three general models at any given time.

A Virtuous Circle

Because of the imbalance in portfolios, some companies have been able to monetize their IP assets in spectacular fashion. IBM, Qualcomm, and Texas Instruments are three good examples. Today, aggregate company IP licensing revenues are in the hundreds of billions of dollars. Some companies also leverage their IP in other important ways. In addition to freedom of action or monetary gain, thoughtful companies consider tax advantages, use of IP to create standards to enhance future product or competitive positions (with or without royalty structures), and the use of the portfolio in conjunction with important business or political relationships. It's all about leverage and the ability to use the portfolio to enhance tactical and strategic choices for a business.

Let's posit your company is beginning to enjoy the benefits of a licensing program. Still, you wake up one morning asking yourself if more can be done to generate returns. By now, this may have become an important question, because the CEO and CFO have come to appreciate the return to the bottom line from licensing, which has produced an unexpected source of income and a return on your company's existing R&D effort. The short answer is "yes," more can (and arguably should) be done, although it will again diverge from what most executives and boards consider common sense.

Licensing activities and how they are perceived can be greatly enhanced with the addition of another form of IP—trade secrets or know-how—usually in the form of technology transfer. Patent licensing focuses largely on the past. It generally seeks royalties for uses that are already apparent. In contrast, know-how licensing focuses on the future. It transfers technologies, allowing the licensee faster access to markets while reducing its R&D expense. The fundamental rule or default position is that all technology or know-how should be available for license, at the right time and under the right terms. The right terms just might include a patent license covering the manufacture, use, or sale of the technology at issue, or it may be broader. For a useful invention, there should be many parties who would benefit from licensing both the underlying patent(s) and the know-how to jump-start market entry.

There is, however, an important distinction with a patent licensing program. Although it is possible to generalize a patent licensing program within a company, this cannot be the course for know-how or technology licensing. For the latter to work effectively, the following must be understood: a solid assessment of where the company's strategic interests lie, the industry's competitive landscape, the barriers to entry in the industry, your sustainable advantage, the possibility of broader adoption, and the business case. Even when a decision is made to move ahead and license a particular technology, the licensing company may have to pony up resources to make the transfer workable for the transferee. This obligation may continue for an extended period for the program to be effective. In short, these types of decisions cannot be made lightly.

There are important second-order effects from trade secret licensing:

- It can lead to adoption of your technology as a de facto industry standard.
- It will help defray the R&D costs for subsequent generations of the technology.
- It can serve as recognition for the developers and researchers involved in creating the technology. It will force them to stay on their toes for your company to have any expectation the licensee will return for subsequent bites of the apple. It motivates continued innovation.
- If you do not license your trade secrets and know-how, it is a good bet your competition will. So, the important question for

management is: Are they willing to accept eventual loss of position or will they seize the moment?

For most companies, it is unrealistic to expect such broad-based technology licensing programs to develop from the ground up. Nor will they easily occur by executive mandate alone. Fear and resistance down the line will only ensure a slow death of the best-intended edict. Rather, these sophisticated programs require education and buy-in, up and down the line. They require a strong corporate commitment to the requisite follow-through, if for no other reason than because your corporate reputation is at stake. Licensing programs are powerful engines that can have considerable impact on your company's behavior and its bottom line, to say nothing of the effects beyond your company.

FIGURE 2.2

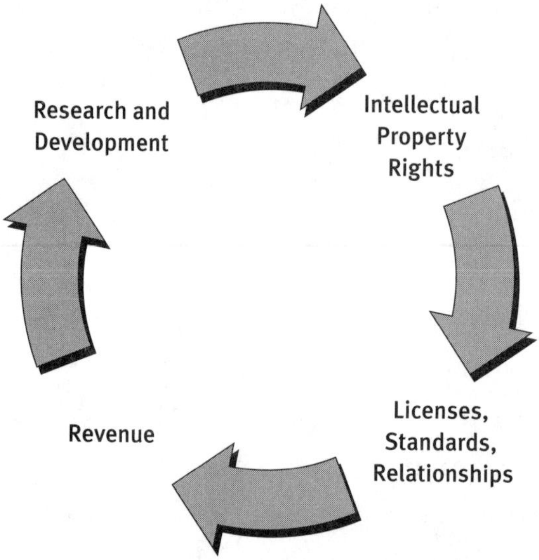

Research and Development

Intellectual Property Rights

Revenue

Licenses, Standards, Relationships

A Virtuous Circle. A good way to visualize the impact of patent licensing on an information technology company is to consider a circle. Through licensing patents and selected know-how (trade secrets) a company can help to generate royalties, set industry standards, establish business relationships and fund R&D activities. These activities, in turn, fuel more licensing.

One good way to think about the effects within a company is to view licensing as an element of a virtuous circle (Figure 2.2).

By licensing its patents and selected know-how (trade secrets), a company can, in addition to generating revenue, help set industry standards, establish business relationships, and fund superior R&D activities, which, in turn, fuel more high-margin licensing.

Starting with the company's R&D investment, a well-run program is likely to create important intellectual property. Subsumed into a licensing program, that IP can generate revenues and profits (and other important benefits as described previously). This revenue returns to the company, and the circle begins anew. Of course, the second-order effect of the outlicensing program is the creation of downstream ecosystems with their own virtuous circles, and on and on.

Four Keys to an Effective Licensing Program

Here are four tips on how to get a licensing program started and pitfalls to avoid:

1. **As you begin any licensing endeavor, make sure you have the goods.** Ensure that whatever you are licensing has substantial value in the marketplace. If you are licensing old or unimportant technologies, expect to fail. If the patent portfolio is flabby or comes with issues, expect to fail. There will certainly be hard scrutiny in any due diligence process. My advice is to conduct an investigation yourself, first. Imagine that you are on the other end of the transaction. (This is not poker; bluffing is not allowed.)

2. **A good way to get a quick start is to find a P&L in your company that needs help.** Successful P&Ls will be less receptive to being audacious in this area. However, a struggling unit may be just what you need. So lead by example.

3.   **The more you are able to centralize the management of IP licensing within your company, the better off you will be.** Multiple programs covering similar aspects and subject matter will only result in a race to the bottom. Different programs are fine for GE with 11 large, separate, and distinct P&Ls, but how many GEs are there?

4.   **It is important to align motivations and incentives within a company for any licensing program to succeed.** Sales managers typically are compensated based on increasing market share and maintaining margins, not on return on R&D. Managers must participate in the upside of licensing activities.

INNOVATIVE USES FOR INNOVATION RIGHTS

Licensing programs that are as financially successful as those run by Texas Instruments or Qualcomm are rare. However, any company doing state-of-the-art R&D, irrespective of size, owes it to its stakeholders to ensure that its assets are fully utilized. Licensing is all about leverage. IP can be used to support businesses in many ways, including trading with others, licensing to others, providing protection, allowing freedom of action, relationship building, and standards development. In the horse-trading of individual patents, families of patents, and know-how, there are infinite variations, with diverse royalty and payment schemes. They reflect the "perceived value" of the property being traded between parties, but, in every case, relevant R&D and appropriate legal rights are being passed into the ecosystem. Each use will have a direct or indirect impact on the company's bottom line—as will doing nothing with your IP.

Most of this chapter has featured the positive side of licensing; indeed, I believe the positives greatly outweigh the negatives. But there may come a time when, because of newness, unfamiliarity with licensing in your industry, or difficulty on the part of others, a heavier-handed approach is required. This means the specter of litigation. Although patent litigation is inherently unpredictable, time consuming, unedifying, expensive, and represents a considerable personal commitment for employees and management, it is sometimes necessary. This assumes you have the goods that the other party actually needs a license from you to proceed, and you are prepared to follow through to the conclusion. You may need to spend millions of dollars and many years accomplishing your result, but you may discover it is the only way to get the industry to take you seriously and bring your licensing program to fruition. Many patentees large and small have found this to be a fact.

An affirmative outlicensing program is a vehicle to directly enhance stakeholder value. Remember, most companies invest in R&D irrespective of the existence of an affirmative outlicensing program. Failure to engage in a broad outlicensing program is to ignore perhaps the best available vehicle for high-percentage bottom-line profits. Often, licensing is a "gross equals net" business, where the difference between the two reflects the tiny cost of running the licensing program. Ninety-five percent net margins are not unusual in an active patent licensing program. Smart companies know how to deliver performance and shareholder value. A licensing program can be a company's most effective resource for doing so.

The fact is, that one new idea leads to another,
and that to a third, and so on through a course
of time until someone, with whom no one of these
ideas was original, combines all together, and
produces what is justly called a new invention.

—Thomas Jefferson, Director of
First U.S. Patent Board, circa 1813

Seeing through the Illusion of Exclusion

BY DANIEL P. McCURDY

Profile: Purveyor of Quality

When Dan McCurdy was a boy growing up in Greensboro, North Carolina, he liked to collect things. When he should have been out playing high school sports, he hung around flea markets and junk shops looking for buried treasure—old pottery, gold pocket watches, early American furniture. Often, his wanderings led to a tidy profit. "It didn't take me long to determine that with a little digging you could identify all sorts of overlooked things that some people valued more than others," recalls McCurdy.

Dan McCurdy and Millie, an English Spaniel, at their house in Bucks County, Pennsylvania.

Today, McCurdy is CEO of ThinkFire, a three-year-old intellectual property licensing and consulting business that partners with companies to maximize value. Marshall Phelps, former vice president of intellectual property for IBM in its formative licensing years and current chief IP strategist at Microsoft, and Nathan Myhrvold, former chief technology officer at Microsoft, both were early board members of ThinkFire.

Because it often seeks licenses on behalf of its clients, ThinkFire is sometimes mistaken for a patent predator, but the company does not buy patents to enforce. Instead, it advises its clients on the *business* issues surrounding intellectual property, working closely with their in-house IP professionals and lawyers. ThinkFire constructs patent defenses as well as identifies recovery opportunities. Like IBM, Lucent, Philips, Thomson, Texas Instruments, and others, it seeks to help clients maximize returns on inventions that have known value and to minimize payments to others. *Forbes* reported in October 2004 that at the time ThinkFire had a pipeline filled with some $300 million in potential patent royalties, a figure McCurdy says has increased significantly.

"There really are few Rembrandts in the attic," says McCurdy. "Mostly there are moths; the masterpieces are displayed in museums. Companies usually know where to find their best intellectual property. But even when you know where they are, the work required to extract additional value from them is intricate. Carrying some of that burden is where ThinkFire fits in."

Before starting ThinkFire, McCurdy served as president of Lucent Technologies' Intellectual Property Business and chairman of Lucent's intellectual property licensing subsidiaries. In 2000 this group generated more than $500 million in annual licensing revenues for Lucent. As head of Lucent's patent licensing and patent creation operations (employing more than 300 licensing professionals and attorneys), McCurdy was responsible for its 600 worldwide patent license agreements derived from more than 26,000 patents.

A political science and history graduate of the University of North Carolina, McCurdy's first job was working for the Governor of North Carolina on high-tech economic development projects for the state. He then joined IBM in Washington, D.C., in the global government affairs office, before launching into a series of assignments within

IBM in marketing, sales, and product management. After having advised IBM government officials negotiating global agreements, such as the GATT TRIPS agreement, he emerged as an expert in the intersection between intellectual property issues and business. When he was subsequently assigned as Director of Business Development to help IBM's famed research division extract revenue from its intellectual property, he put his diverse experience to use. After 15 years with IBM, McCurdy left to diversify his business experience. "I didn't want to be seventy years old and look back on my life as having made only safe choices," he says.

"I get bored easily," says McCurdy with characteristic candor. "The IP business is great for me because it is complex and always changing. You need to move around a lot to keep up with the landscape."

Says one of his Fortune 500 clients: "Dan is a strategist who speaks the language of the business executive, as well as that of the patent attorney and engineer." He often advises CEOs, CFOs, and boards of directors, and helps their licensing executives and IP directors facilitate dialogue with them.

When McCurdy is not working and traveling extensively for business, he likes to run, lift weights, practice yoga, and cook in his 1840 Bucks County, Pennsylvania stone home. He also enjoys hiking with his four English cocker spaniels. His interest in accumulating undervalued furnishings has not waned. Paintings, rugs, and 17th-century American furniture are his primary focus. He stays politically active and sits on Solebury Township's Planning Commission. President Clinton's chief of staff and key technology advisor, John Podesta, is a member of ThinkFire's advisory board.

The illusion of exclusion (i.e., of patent exclusivity), which he writes about in the following chapter, is something that McCurdy believes obscures many smart managers' thinking. Patents provide a technical period of exclusivity, which, in practice, is far less extensive, more fleeting, and difficult to enforce than companies realize. It is only a matter of time before shareholders notice.

A seismic shift is taking place in the way inventions and the rights that protect them are viewed by the world's most innovative companies. After 20 years of debate and dissection, old intellectual property management models—based on the development of defensive patent portfolios designed to exclude others rather than to generate revenue—are no longer sustainable. They involve too much expense and time and do not contribute enough to overall goals.

In the past, patent licensing was largely the game of huge market players licensing one another to their respective patents or, occasionally, the result of infringement lawsuits. On very rare occasions, a "Rembrandt" (a patent masterpiece found in someone's moldy attic) found its way into the licensing world on the end of a big stick, resulting in significant cash to the expeditionary who discovered it.

Today, IP licensing is undergoing a profound transformation, as potential licensees demand more from IP transactions than simply a license to an allegedly infringed patent. Increasingly, potential licensees are seeking from licensors a deal that can bring them significant value, rather than simply taxing the revenues the licensee currently enjoys. Similarly, smart licensors are attempting to uncover business relationships or assets the licensee might benefit from that can bring the licensor more value than a royalty alone. Unlike the traditional win-lose scenarios (win for the licensor, lose for the licensee), which were the dominant patent licensing relationships of the past, win–win scenarios will increasingly dominate the business landscape of the future.

The result could ultimately be companies opening up their entire technology and IP portfolio to competitors as long as the terms and the timing of the deal are right. Companies like IBM that follow an active IP management strategy are reaping large rewards, whereas those that choose to continue to pursue a defensive strategy, much to shareholders' detriment, will never realize the full potential of what they own. The stage is being set for companies to make a conscious, public choice about the role played by their intangible assets, especially patents, in determining their future. Failure of senior management to identify and fully deploy their companies' innovations, and to link them masterfully to the firm's strategy and business plans, will not go unnoticed by competitors or shareholders.

IP ON THE RADAR SCREEN

For most of the 20th century, IP management was the purview of patent lawyers working in the back rooms of major corporations. Patents were filed, first and foremost, to protect the company's products from being pilfered by others with ambitions to copy or closely imitate their products. Companies that engaged in copycat activity circumvented R&D costs and thereby increased profitability dramatically. Although competition was present during this period, the pressure from global powerhouses seeking lucrative markets was less intense.

As global competition and investment in R&D increased during the 1980s, firms began to explore the use of intellectual property to enhance their competitiveness. Companies desired the ability to produce any product that emerged from their R&D activities without fear of having others block the manufacturing or sale of those products with a proprietary patent position. This idea was conceived and flourished during the Cold War, when the strategy of mutually assured destruction as a mechanism to deter the threat of nuclear annihilation was born. The theory was to build a nuclear arsenal large enough to destroy those who would first launch against you, and you would diminish the threat. Nuclear arsenals thus grew significantly among the national superpowers, while nuclear proliferation was somewhat contained through diplomatic, economic, and technological means.

Similarly, as a result of this intention to deter others from patent attacks, companies began to build significant patent arsenals of their own. "Launch against me, and I will launch back," they seemed to say. Both companies would sustain enormous economic damage, so stability was achieved because neither wanted such a war. From 1965 through 1985, USPTO patent applications and grants remained relatively constant, with patents granted averaging about 50,000 per year and applications averaging about 70,000 per year. In about 1985, applications began to skyrocket, and with the exception of a dramatic drop in 1995 to 1996, they grew from about 70,000 applications in 1985 to more than 175,000 by 2001. Issued patents doubled from about 45,000 in 1985 to almost 90,000 by 2001.

Many have criticized this so-called patent arms race (and clearly— as with all arms races—it has come with considerable expense). Notwithstanding this expense, it is likely that the fears that the competition fueled inventions that may not have been as important or worthwhile to corporate investment did not deter the participants. Thus, we were off and running in a global technological race, driven by both competition and fear: fear of loss of market share, fear of technological obsolescence, and fear of being placed in a box by those with superior patent positions. Being careful was more important than being right.

GAINING COMPETITIVE ADVANTAGE

While many firms continued to build their IP portfolios, others lagged behind. Some felt that the patent system actually inhibited invention, rather than enhanced it, believing that inventions should be shared. This was perhaps a precursor to elements of today's Open Source movement. Others never built a patenting culture whereby technologists were encouraged to seek a patent on their important inventions. Still others were convinced that building a portfolio was a justifiable investment, but they did not have the financial resources to do so. From 1985 to the present, patent haves and patent have-nots clearly emerged, not to mention those that were unable to utilize their large patent arsenals effectively, as was the case with many Japanese companies. There were at least two primary reasons for the failure of companies with arsenals: (1) decentralized patent management and (2) an unwillingness to strike first as a defensive measure when it was perceived that a patent attack from specific entities was inevitable.

Even among companies that successfully built large patent arsenals, many did not know when to stop and invested more than was necessary to achieve freedom of action, licensing success, or any other IP objective (except perhaps making the inventor happy that she or he could add another patent to the collection). Although size counts, a bigger patent portfolio is not always a better one. The key is to have a significant portfolio in size, but to focus on the quality of the patents, claim construction, avoidability, detectability, probable market impact, and so on.

IBM Leads the Way

By the late 1980s, with the patent arms race well underway, and with the IP and competitive landscape evolving, IP techniques began to change. This was driven more by the patent haves, led by IBM, than the patent have-nots.

IBM's history in intellectual property was the result of an unusual past. Guided in significant part by the 1956 Consent Decree ending anti-trust litigation with the U.S. government, IBM agreed to license any patent it owned to anyone who requested a license under fair, reasonable, and nondiscriminatory terms. The idea, presumably, was to remove IBM's ability to use its patents to perpetuate its market position. Other companies, such as Xerox, had been dealt even worse blows by the U.S. government on the patent front, demonstrating a total lack of understanding by the government at that time of the linkage between a strong patent system, innovation, and competitiveness.

For decades following the Consent Decree, IBM and other large corporations perfected the use of their patent portfolios to achieve freedom of action. But over time, as its dominance over the industry waned in the face of increased global competition, IBM became both more aggressive and more inventive, with respect to the use of its IP portfolio.

While broad patent cross-licenses continued to be pursued, IBM came to expect a significant "balancing payment" to compensate for the strength of its portfolio versus the strength of the portfolio owned by the cross-licensee. Other companies continued to hold to the view that a "zero-zero cross" was best (a license in which two parties agree to license one another to their respective patent portfolios, with no dollars changing hands). These licenses at that time were frequently for the life of all patents subject to the license that had been issued as of the effective date of the license agreement.

Over time, IBM learned that it could achieve significant financial success in licensing its patent portfolio for profit because the expenses related to the licensing of patents—particularly absent litigation—are extremely small relative to the royalties received (net margins generally exceed 90%, versus 10% on many products). A successful licensing business can, therefore, have a dramatic and disproportionately positive impact on profitability and stock price. Five hundred million dollars in licensing revenues is roughly equivalent to the profit contribution of $4.5 billion in product sales with a 10% net contribution margin.

However, companies also discovered that patent enforcement as a stand-alone engagement is a slow and painful process. So, during the dark days of IBM, when many were questioning the company's survival, IBM was still recognized for its technological strength. IBM also needed cash. With many, many tens of billions of dollars in R&D expenses over the prior decade, IBM remained rich in technological know-how, including specialized semi-conductor designs and manufacturing processes, novel ways to make storage disk drives, and even how to make lasers for the ablation of human tissue (the fundamental technology used for corneal sculpting today).

IBM hypothesized that approaching companies with the opportunity to transfer powerful technologies to them that they could use to make money, and also licensing IBM's patent portfolio for use both in the transferred technology as well as other products offered by the licensee, was not only more lucrative, but also dramatically faster to achieve. Licensing a proven technology enables the licensee to make money, as opposed to taking away money they have already made. Over a period of a decade, IBM grew its licensing revenues to more than $1.7 billion annually, with royalties from the licensing of patents taking second chair to royalties derived from the transfer and licensing of technology (the know-how underlying patents).

Notwithstanding this success, many companies—suffering from what can be termed the "illusion of exclusion"—failed to adopt and actively pursue the licensing of valuable patents and technologies. They believed that the market exclusivity afforded by their key patents and distinguishing technologies was more valuable (and sustainable) than the profit margins that might be realized from selectively licensing them. Instead, they searched for hidden treasures, rather than the masterpieces under their noses that were already the basis for their own product successes.

Timing the License

The illusion of exclusion is among the most treacherous and dangerous myths involving intellectual property. It pervades (and corrupts) licensing thought in most industries and companies. The misconception is that if a company possesses highly differentiating technologies that provide its products or services with a competitive edge, licensing those technologies to others would be suicidal. This belief is fallacious on multiple fronts.

First, there are almost always multiple technological means available or discoverable to achieve the same or similar results. Even in life sciences, where exclusion was once thought to be essential, increased R&D regularly produces multiple means to achieve a similar biological intervention (examples include anti-acid medications Prevacid® vs. Nexium® and Viagra® vs. Levitra®). Thus, if a market is sufficiently promising, competition will always drive companies to find an alternative means to participate in that market. It is a misconception that it is self-destructive for companies with highly differentiating technologies that provide a competitive edge to license them to others (Figure 3.1).

When a company discovers and perfects a technology, substance, or process, rather than keeping everything to itself, that company should immediately give thought to licensing the invention to others (at the

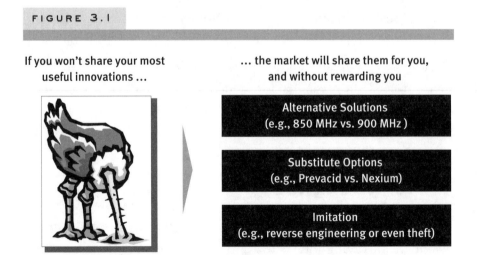

FIGURE 3.1

If you won't share your most useful innovations ...

... the market will share them for you, and without rewarding you

Alternative Solutions
(e.g., 850 MHz vs. 900 MHz)

Substitute Options
(e.g., Prevacid vs. Nexium)

Imitation
(e.g., reverse engineering or even theft)

The Illusion of Exclusion. Companies with highly differentiating technologies that provide a competitive edge are not committing suicide by licensing the invention to others.

right time, under the right terms). Doing this not only allows the company to access that portion of the market into which not even the most dominant of technologies can find its way, but also allows the company to maintain its R&D lead and to ensure that its technology becomes the de facto industry standard.

Determining the timing of a license is more difficult than determining the terms. If the technology is licensed too early, competition may be introduced too soon, driving down market share and/or profit margins prematurely. If the technology is licensed too late, potential licensees will be too invested in their own competing technologies to abandon them. Finding the right balance in timing is essential. Remember, the lead time is at least a couple of years given the time required to negotiate a license, transfer the technology to the licensee, for the licensee to manufacture the product, and integrate it into its sales and distribution channel.

The process of finding this balance is never achieved by ignoring the potential licensing opportunities. It is critical for every company to maintain a current inventory of its most valuable technologies, generally identifiable as those that (1) are known by the industry to be leading technologies; (2) have been proven by use in the company's successful products or services; (3) are capable of being transferred to others, generally by engineers, technologists, and/or manufacturing staffs teaching their counterparts designated by the licensee; (4) are serving significant and growing markets; and (5) that are being continually invested in and refreshed by the company so that its leading technological position can be maintained. Innovation ensures a constant flow of new and improved technologies to the licensee and a perpetual flow of royalties to the licensing company.

Once this inventory is initially developed—and is established as a normal part of corporate planning and product management processes, operations reviews, and strategy activities—management should assess the business case behind whether, when, and under what terms each of the most promising technologies might be licensed. Again, remembering that licensing too soon may be detrimental to the business case, and too late may result in potential licensees being too invested in alternatives to consider a license.

KNOWING WHAT YOU HAVE

The key is that knowing what you have to license is a distinct decision from whether you license it! If, by way of example, your company has 80% market share in a product with 25% net margins, and you project that it will be five years before anyone can create an alternative to the technology driving that product's success (a rare occurrence), licensing the technology at that moment would be foolish. If, however, you believe that five years hence a competing product will almost certainly be possible, and that when it is introduced, margins will be driven to 10% from 25% (and that it will take potential licensees three or more years to actually receive your technology and place it in products in the market), it may well make sense to enter into licensing discussions in one year, seeking a royalty of at least 10% (perhaps 5% to 6% for the technology and 4% to 5% for patents needed to practice the technology). This will hopefully be soon enough to avert significant investment by the licensee(s) in alternative technologies, thereby providing the environment for them to take a license and positioning your company for competition in the same time frame in which it would have occurred anyway. Rather than being trampled by this new competition, you have positioned your company to benefit from it through royalties.

Successful patent licensing programs can, and in many cases should, go hand-in-hand with successful products (Figure 3.2). Marginal or failed inventions are not likely to yield substantial licenses. Frequently,

EXHIBIT 3.2

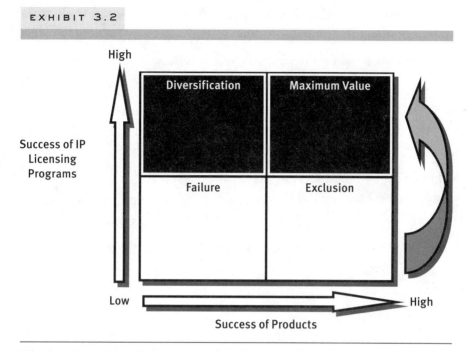

Winning, Even When You Lose. Successful patent licensing programs can, and in many cases should, go hand-in-hand with successful products. Marginal or failed inventions are not likely to yield substantial licenses. Most high-tech patents have surprisingly short useful lives.

patents have surprisingly short useful lives. Properly timed licensing maximizes the profitability of an invention and can expand its impact.

The point is simple: Even the most successful companies can seldom maintain a majority share of the market. Alternative solutions are developed, and clients buy from others for many reasons. Multiple factors beyond technology strength contribute to success in the market: manufacturing efficiencies, access to capital, distribution advantages, differences in the nature of comprehensive solutions, and personal relationships, to name a few. By licensing technologies at the right time under the right terms, your company can actually win in the market (through receipt of royalties) even when it loses the sale. Moreover, strategic licensing can drive adoption of your technologies as a de facto standard, further driving competitive advantages you might enjoy, as well as enhancing revenue streams as others license and use your technology. It is crucial to recognize that these techniques work with your best technologies, not your worst.

All of this seems simple on paper, but there are real challenges in getting such a program introduced into a business—which explains why so few have embraced it up to now. IBM is not completely alone; others such as Procter & Gamble and BT in the United Kingdom also, to some extent at least, have similar models, and companies such as Hewlett Packard and even Microsoft are beginning to look at the idea. The fact is the license "everything" policy has not so far found widespread support. It is only fair to ask why not?

Masterpieces Hang in Museums, Not in Attics

Most companies know their best technologies, products, and services. The market adopts them, they become successful, and they generate substantial revenue and profit. They are driving the company's business forward and are far from hidden away.

The problem is that, because of the illusion of exclusion, companies have traditionally been reluctant to license their best technologies. Hearing of the licensing success of companies like IBM and Texas Instruments, CEOs and CFOs around the world encourage their management to achieve similar financial results from licensing programs. People are hired, money is invested, years pass, but success is elusive. Business leaders and the licensing staff become discouraged, and after tens or hundreds of millions of dollars of R&D investment, they throw in the towel.

This occurs because the licensing organization was looking for hidden masterpieces, rather than the treasures hanging in front of them on their walls. This is likely because business management did not come to terms with the illusion of exclusion. They refused to allow their best technologies to be licensed at the right time under the right terms, and they sent the licensing staff on a scavenger hunt to deploy noncore technologies that had not been proven, or misfit technologies, or rejected technologies. What is most sad is that after attempts to license the company's best junk fails, they conclude that licensing does not work. The trick is to see through the illusion of exclusion so that the need to find those Rembrandts, which in almost all cases never materialize, will not be necessary. The licensing organization will be too busy negotiating and closing deals and counting money to visit the flea market.

EMERGING MODELS

Traditional ways of managing IP are no longer effective. Companies need to identify their best intellectual property and use this property to leverage better deals that accomplish their strategic and tactical needs. This may involve incoming royalties, improved distribution models, lower prices from suppliers, increased purchases from customers, increased cooperation in mutually beneficial standards, or many other facets that bring value to both licensor and licensee (of course, always attentive to and compliant with procompetitive activities). This new approach does not require that your best know-how or trademarks be licensed, but it does require knowledge of the IP assets that might be used to help accomplish value-producing corporate objectives. Whether to use any given asset is a cost-benefit analysis that is specific to the case at hand. Sometimes, having a strong patent position may, alone, be enough; other times, it will not be.

The new approaches to IP may not be perfect for every company, but depending on their industry and particular product lines, these approaches cannot be ignored by most companies without peril. Companies with strong patents and successful products can make a lot of money from using their best IP wisely. If they do not, they may be doomed to spend too much for too little reward. Underpinning all approaches is a simple truth: If the invention and the patent or patents that read on it are good enough, both parties will be interested in finding a deal that works for you and for them. After all, winning is more fun than losing.

*A*n ironmonger in London [in 1742], however,
assuming a good deal of my pamphlet, and working
it up into his own, and making some small changes
in the machine, which rather hurt its operation, got
a patent for it there, and made, as I was told, a little
fortune by it. And this is not the only instance of
patents taken out for my inventions by others, tho' not
always with the same success, which I never contested,
as having no desire of profiting by patents myself,
and hating disputes.

—Benjamin Franklin, 1771

On Patent Trolls
and Other Myths

BY ALEXANDER POLTORAK

Profile: Knight in Shining Armor

As a Soviet dissident, Alexander Poltorak was followed everywhere. The KGB started tracking him at 14 when he spoke out in school about corruption. Later, the Soviets stripped him of his doctoral degree in theoretical physics. Then he came to the United States in 1982. "It was the invasion of Afghanistan and the exile of Sakharov that put me over the top," he recalls. "But emigrating from the former Soviet Union was no cake walk."

Alex Poltorak, Ph.D. physicist, ponders the latest in relativity theory.

When Poltorak arrived in the United States, he served as Assistant Professor of Biomathematics at the Neurology Department of Cornell University Medical College. He conducted research in image processing and computer tomography. Before establishing General Patent Corporation, an IP management and licensing firm, in 1987, Poltorak was CEO of Rapitech

Systems, Inc., then a publicly traded computer company that he co-founded in 1983.

At about this time, he met Steven Farago, a Ph.D. inventor and electrical engineer who had emigrated from Hungary. Rapitech acquired Farago's inventions for smart connectors, the technology underlying PCMCIA or PC cards, with the intention of commercializing them. But after a year of speaking with companies and potential customers, the pair found that the inventions were already being produced without permission.

"There was little we could do to stimulate sales of our products when big companies were already manufacturing them, so we decided to point out the inventions were not theirs to use. No one believed that a tiny company like ours would actually be able to successfully sue them." The Farago saga was featured in a 2001 article in *Inventors Digest,* entitled "Patent Enforcement: To Sue or Not to Sue."

With Poltorak's help, Farago decided to turn up the heat about enforcing the rights to the smart card connectors. Today, there are 130 licensees of the Farago smart card patents worth in the tens of millions of dollars. Because no company wants to pay money it does not believe it has to, the Rapitech patents were reexamined by the U.S. Patent and Trademark Office in 2003 to 2004. All claims were upheld and unamended. "This result actually strengthened our patent position with regard to licensing other companies," notes Poltorak.

"Patents are not worth anything if they are infringed but unenforced," says Poltorak, whose father was an appellate judge in Russia. "Unfortunately, most investors are not in the position to do anything about it. A patent is the right to sue—a pretty empty threat if an inventor or company does not have sufficient resources to back it up."

Like some contingency attorneys, Poltorak views his organization, which today has more than a dozen clients, as the champion of the little guy and the independent inventor—an upholder of the system. "We don't buy patents or speculate on them like some companies. We do, however, share our success with inventors. Where some companies may see a 'troll,' inventors tell us they see a 'knight in shining armor'."

Poltorak is the author of IP best-sellers *Essentials of Intellectual Property* and *Essentials of Intellectual Property Licensing*, which he co-wrote with General Patent Corp. general counsel, Paul Lerner. In his spare time, Poltorak continues to do research in relativity theory and is an adjunct professor of business law at the Globe Institute of Technology in New York. In addition to Intellectual Property Owners and the Licensing Executives Society, he is a member of the International Society for General Relativity and Gravitation and the American Association for the Advancement of Science. A profile of him, entitled "Trying to Cash In on Patents," appeared in *The New York Times* in 2002.

In his chapter "On Patent Trolls and Other Myths," Poltorak waxes poetic about the strange folklore that some companies have perpetuated about enforcing patents. He provides some basic advice to both infringers and the infringed.

Fear of the unknown, has spawned legends and myths that make up the folklore of nations. So, too, does the folklore of the modern corporation have its myths. Few images are more frightening than an injunction-threatening, damages-demanding patent holder. The arcane and oft-misunderstood world of intellectual property casts expressionistic shadows on the ravages of patent enforcement.

Many myths have been told in the patent wonderland. Today, corporate fathers read their children scary stories before kissing them goodnight, the stories about demon patent trolls that terrorize the noble

Source: Elana and Walter Borowski/PNI

Tall Tales. The popular children's story *Little Red Riding Hood* contains many thematic components common to the legend or myth: a young heroine undergoes trials and obstacles, good and evil characters are clearly-defined opposites, and the heroine receives help in the form of magic. A fairy tale may survive many generations through its retelling.

business folk. Instead of nursery rhymes (Figure 4.1), the corporate dads read their children the *Ballad of the Patent Troll.* It goes something like this:

> *On the road of innovation*
> *Sits an ugly Patent Troll.*
> *From the largest corporations*
> *He extorts a Patent Toll.*
>
> *Armed with mighty patent claims,*
> *Claiming willfulness and tort,*
> *Treble damages and pains*
> *He drags infringers into court.*

> *Your resistance is futile*
> *Patent Troll is strong and vile.*
> *Wielding claim as an ax*
> *He'll exact his patent tax.*
>
> *Corporations, be united!*
> *He who slays the Patent Troll,*
> *By the Queen he will be knighted*
> *And exalted by us all.*

As much as I find these stories enthralling, and despite the protest of the poet in me, I will debunk these myths so that children can sleep at night without fear.

A PATENT IS A NEGATIVE RIGHT

It is useful to review the definition of patent trolls. Peter Detkin, who coined the expression during his tenure as Intel's patent counsel, which he has since modified, defined the patent troll as someone who buys a patent for enforcement purposes but does not practice the patented invention. "'We were sued for libel for the use of the term 'patent extortionists' so I came up with '*patent trolls*,' Detkin said. 'A *patent troll* is somebody who tries to make a lot of money off a patent that they are not practicing and have no intention of practicing and in most cases never practiced.'"[1] (Other terms used are patent *vulture*, bottom feeders, pirates, and *terrorist*, not to mention *canis filius*.[2]) This definition implies that to be a legitimate patent owner, among other things, the owner must practice his or her invention. The term patent troll also implies, as Bruce Berman points out in his *IP Investor* column

---

[1] Brenda Sandburg, "Inventor's lawyer makes a pile from patents," *The Recorder,* July 30, 2001.

[2] It means "son of a female dog" but sounds less caustic in Latin.

"Illegitimate Assertions?," an image of a subhuman species who "bottom-fishes" by dragging its hook low in the water or casting its net widely, thereby trolling the waters in the hope of landing practically anything of value. In real estate, equities, and other areas of tangible investment, wise bottomfishers, like Warren Buffett, are considered heroes.

Myth #1: "A patent is needed to practice the invention."

Many inventors believe that they need a patent in order to practice their invention. In fact, nothing could be further from the truth. Nobody needs a patent in order to practice an invention. Most companies produce goods for which they do not have a patent or the patent has expired. A patent does not give the patentee the right to practice the patented invention. It confers no positive rights. A patent is strictly a negative or exclusionary right. A patent gives the patentee the right to exclude others from using, making, selling, offering for sale, or importing the patented invention.

How does this myth affect the notion of the patent troll? A patent troll is someone who does not practice the invention protected by the patent he or she owns; it implies that a patent owned by someone who practices the invention differs from a so-called paper patent owned by someone who does not practice the teachings of the patent. Because a patent does not confer on the patentee the right to practice his or her own invention, the patent right has nothing to do with whether or not the inventor practices his or her invention. Consequently, the whole notion of a paper patent has no basis in patent law.[3]

---

[3] Only in the measure of damages does the law differentiate between the patentee who practices the patented invention, who may under certain circumstances be entitled to lost profits, and a patentee enforcing a paper patent who is only entitled to reasonable royalties.

Noble corporate folk sue each other on paper patents without any hesitation. A patent infringement lawsuit brought by Kodak against Sun Microsystems is a recent example of this phenomenon. Kodak sued Sun for infringing Java patents that Kodak inherited from Wang Laboratories. Kodak, as it is well known, is not in the software business. This fact did not stop Kodak from collecting $95 million from Sun. So much for the nobility of the corporate folk.

Myth #2: "It is not 'nice' to sue for patent infringement."

As an exclusionary right, a patent is nothing but a license to sue or an option to bring an action for infringement. It has no other function. Consequently, to blame inventors for suing infringers of their patents is at best disingenuous, because suing is what patents are for! As the ancient said, *Damnant quod non intellegunt* (i.e., "They condemn what they do not understand.").

Moreover, a corporate officer or director who is aware of an infringement of some patents owned by his or her company and who fails to enforce these patents may be held liable for breach of the duty of care with respect to the management of corporate assets.[4] In fact, corporate folks sue each other for patent infringement like it was going out of style. Corporate attorneys schooled in Latin take the position enunciated by the Romans, *Quod licet Iovi, non licet bovi* (i.e., "What Jupiter may do, the ox may not."). To this the inventor not schooled in classics cleverly retorts: "What is good for the goose is good for the gander."

Patent licenses are of two kinds: the so-called carrot (voluntary) licenses and stick (compulsory) licenses. The former are lately exalted by the gurus of management consulting as the way to monetize their

---

[4] See more on this topic in A. Poltorak and P. Lerner, "Corporate Officers and Directors May Be Liable for Mismanagement of Intellectual Property," *Patent Strategy & Management,* May and June 2000.

intellectual assets. They proudly announce that IBM alone derives $1 billion in licensing revenues annually. This is deemed a good thing. Stick licensing, however, is held to be bad medicine. Truth be told, every carrot license is a stick license in disguise. (In the patent wonderland, these disguises are quite common.) Indeed, who would ever license a patent (and pay for it) if not for the fear of a possible patent infringement suit? If good fences make good neighbors, good patents make good partners.

In the good ol' days, the noble folks used to duel over such deplorable offenses as the theft of intellectual property. Back then, ideas were held in high esteem. Nowadays, people go to court. Sabers have been exchanged for patents and pistols for legal briefs. It may be less romantic but no less noble. If we do it more often, perhaps ideas will be held in high esteem once again.

Myth #3: "The value of a patent is the same as the value of the patented technology."

Many patent valuation consultants make the not-so-subtle mistake of equating the value of the patented technology (the invention or any products derived from it) with the value of the patent that protects it. Like the wizards of old, they start with valuing a patent, distract your attention for a moment with wizardly math, and then, by slight of hand, substitute the patent for the technology it protects. Anything goes in the patent wonderland. This is nothing short of absurd no matter how wizardly it may be. Both in law and economics, a patent is a state-sanctioned monopoly granted in exchange for disclosure, and its value is the incremental value of the enhanced cash flows resulting from that monopoly.

The patent and the product covered by it live two separate lives. The patent has little to do with the patented product, besides protecting the monopoly afforded to the product by virtue of the patent; and the product has little to do with the patent that protects it. A strong patent does not necessarily reflect a successful invention, and many successful inventions are covered by patents that are not worth the paper they are printed on. Many products are introduced to the marketplace well before the patents protecting them issue from the patent office, and many continue their commercial life well after the patent expires. The value of the technology is mainly determined by its desirability and competitive advantage (i.e., market demand). The value of the patent, however, depends on completely different questions, namely, (1) how broadly are claims crafted? (2) have they been amended during the prosecution? (3) are there any estoppels in the "file wrapper"? (4) how vigorously is the patent enforced? (5) how easily may its validity be challenged? and (6) how easy is it to design around? This is another illustration that whether or not the patent is practiced is irrelevant to the right to assert the patent.

The value of a patent also depends on the willingness and ability of the patentee to enforce it. The owner of an infringed patent who hesitates to enforce it reduces the value of the patent to zero. It is incumbent on inventors and corporate managers alike to enforce their infringed patents.

Myth #4: "The patent system is fair."

A patent is a bargain between the State and an inventor wherein the inventor is induced to disclose his or her invention by the promise of a limited monopoly (20 years from filing). With the median cost of patent litigation exceeding $2 million, this promise is of little value to a small inventor.

Ironically, the law (35 U.S.C. §112) requires an enabling disclosure from a patentee. This means the patent disclosure must be sufficiently detailed to enable a person with ordinary skills in the art to practice the invention without undue experimentation. However, it does nothing to enable the patentee to enforce his or her exclusionary rights. The inventor upholds his or her end of the bargain by disclosing his or her invention in the patent application, thereby forfeiting a possibly valuable trade secret. By failing to provide the impecunious patentee any effective means of enforcing the patent rights, the State, however, breaches its promise of a limited monopoly for the patentee. (Inventors in R&D departments of companies inevitably "assign" their rights to the company, which is in a much better position both to commercialize inventions and to enforce the rights associated with them.) Independent inventors inevitably get the short end of the stick in this bargain. So much for equality and justice in the patent wonderland.

Aided by this uneven playing field, the noble corporate folks infringe patents owned by helpless independent inventors with impunity. In the good ol' days, it would have been considered vulgar to speak of money among the noble folks. Today, as *U.S. News and World Report* put it, "American justice is the best justice your money can buy." Or, as the late Johnnie Cochran said, "Justice is color-blind—it sees only one color—green."

The only chance inventors have to see justice is to find a law firm or a patent enforcement organization that would take their case on a contingency. To some, these agents, who are seen as patent trolls by the corporate folks, are the angels of hope or the white knights rushing to the rescue of the lonely and downtrodden inventors.

Do Patent Trolls Really Exist?

As previously noted, the accepted definition of a patent troll is someone who buys a patent for enforcement purposes but does not practice the patented invention. It would be silly to argue about a definition. After all, patentees can be their own lexicographer (i.e., they speak in their own language in the patent wonderland). The question is, is this activity wrong or not? As indicated previously, patent law does not distinguish between a patent that is practiced and a patent that is not. Therefore, this notion of a paper patent has no basis either in the law or in economics. All patents are written on paper, regardless if they are practiced.

Having said that, there have been some instances of patent abuse that do not fall into the definition of a patent troll. Submarine patents are the prime example, but they are hardly a threat today. First, depth charges were dropped on them in 1995, when the term of a U.S. patent was changed from 17 years from the date of issue to 20 years from the effective date of filing. It is no longer profitable to delay issuance of patents because that diminishes their remaining life. In 2004, the Federal Circuit ruled them to be unenforceable on the theory of prosecution laches. By and large, submarine patents are a thing of the past.

Those patentees who, like trolls, sit on their patents waiting for damages to accumulate are shooting themselves in the feet. Laches is an effective defense against a patentee who lurks hidden in the bushes (or under the bridge, as trolls do) while an infringer's sales continue to grow.[5] Similarly, patent owners who frivolously assert their patents without any real evidence of infringement, hoping to exact nuisance value settlements, can be sanctioned under Rule 11.

The law has already addressed the difference between a patentee who practices the patented invention and one who does not. The difference is not in the right to assert the patent—they share the same right—but in the remedies available to them. A market participant may be entitled to receive lost profits, whereas a paper patent holder can receive only reasonable royalties, which, typically, are a fraction of the lost profits.

---

[5] How many patent trolls does it take to change a light bulb? None. A patent troll would not change the bulb; he would sit in the darkness waiting for the damages to accumulate.

Just as trolls are mythological figures in Scandinavian folklore, patent trolls are nothing but mythological figures of the corporate folklore.

Myth #5: "A patent is a tax on innovation."

A patent is an intangible asset. Information contained in the patent, once published, can be readily copied and used. This presents what is known in economics as the classic "free rider" problem. A free rider problem is often solved by levying taxes. The army, the police, and your municipal services are all supported by your taxes. The patent system was in part created to solve the free rider problem.

A patent is a bargain between the State and an inventor wherein the inventor discloses his or her invention to the public in exchange for a limited monopoly. The inventor can share this monopoly by way of licensing the patent in consideration of royalty payments—a tax, if you will. A patent may, therefore, be viewed as a form of tax. However, a patent is not a tax on innovation (it is not the inventor who is taxed); it is a tax on the exploitation of innovation created by others. This is not merely semantics. Think of a patent as a toll road on the highway paved by the inventor to a commercialized invention or product. If the manufacturer of the product wants to get from point A to point B via this highway, it is only fair to pay the toll to reward those who have built the road, whatever their out of pocket cost.

In the patent wonderland, there are many myths. Don't scare your children with them. Just kiss them goodnight.

If some one man in a tribe, more sagacious than the others, invented a new snare or weapon, or other means of attack or defense, the plainest self-interest, without the assistance of much reasoning power, would prompt the other members to imitate him; and all would thus profit. The habitual practice of each new art must likewise in some slight degree strengthen the intellect. If the new invention were an important one, the tribe would increase in number, spread, and supplant other tribes.

—Charles Darwin, 1871

Roadblocks, Toll Roads, and Bridges: Using a Patent Portfolio Wisely

BY PETER DETKIN

Profile: From Trolls to Tolls

Peter Detkin may forever be known as the person who coined the term "patent troll." In 2001 Detkin was serving as Director of Licensing and Patent Litigation at Intel Corp. The company had been hit by a rash of patent suits, some frivolous, and Detkin, in fact, characterized asserters as "extortionists." Raymond Niro, a Chicago patent litigator and also a contributor to this book, filed a libel suit on behalf of a client to restrain Detkin's use of the term. Detkin believed that enforcing a patent that the owner does not practice was akin to a shakedown. To Intel, it certainly must have felt that way. "The term had equity value at the time," he says.

Silicon Valley IP Player, Peter Detkin, plays with his dog, Hershey.

Since retiring from Intel in 2003 to join Intellectual Ventures as Managing Director, Detkin has been choosing his words more carefully. Intellectual Ventures, founded by Nathan Myhrvold, former Microsoft Chief Technology Officer, is a company that invents and invests in inventions. They also acquire others' usually unused patents. Intellectual Ventures has been closed-mouthed about its business model, which includes accumulating literally thousands of patents. To date, IV has not asserted against a company and says they have no plans to. "We hold invention workshops and formulate ideas and inventions that we file patent applications on," says Detkin. "Building portfolios of complimentary patents provides value."

In a November 2004 article, *Newsweek* reported that Intellectual Ventures had raised more than $350 million from information technology giants like Microsoft, Intel, Sony, Nokia, and Apple, and added that Google and eBay also had recently invested in the company. Others have put the figure substantially higher. It's anyone's guess how Intellectual Ventures will deploy its patents. One thing is clear, however: they hold a lot of IP rights and will be acquiring more, and they have the experience and vision to know how to monetize them.

Detkin, who grew up outside of New York in suburban Long Island, served as an associate at the IP specialty firm Kenyon & Kenyon in New York before becoming the first patent attorney at the legendary Silicon Valley law firm of Wilson, Sonsini, Goodrich, and Rosato. While there, he held second-chair responsibility for a number of high-profile cases, including the landmark *Lotus v. Borland*. From there he joined Intel, where he spent eight years, eventually heading patent licensing and litigation.

Detkin lives in Los Altos, California, in the heart of Silicon Valley, and has a home in Lake Tahoe, where he skis with his family. He is an avid tennis player and tries to play three times a week. He now works mainly from his home. ("I have the privilege of running a virtual office," he says.) Although he has been a Californian for many years, Detkin is still much the New Yorker. "I had been driving Hondas for years, but someone told me I should get a Lexus, so I thought I had better get one," he says.

For the past seven years, Detkin has devoted a significant part of his workweek to the Law Foundation of Silicon Valley (www.law-foundation.org), and became its president in late 2005. It's an organization dedicated to providing legal services to low-income children and families, people with mental and developmental disabilities, AIDS patients, and victims of discrimination. It serves 6,000 families a year. The board reads like a who's who of Silicon Valley companies and law firms. Detkin is a financial supporter and donates about 10 hours of his time each week to foundation activities.

Detkin's chapter focuses on using patents not just to defend turf, as they have been historically, but as bridges or toll roads that lead not only to profitability but also to business opportunities for companies of all sizes and independent inventors, too.

Most managers think of a patent as a defensive ploy—a "No Trespassing" sign posted to prevent one company from using another's inventions. But using patents as a roadblock is the last thing some companies should be thinking about when it comes to enhancing profitability. Patents can serve as a bridge to generate significant revenue, as well as to facilitate sales and business opportunities. Companies that regard their patent portfolio too narrowly are likely undermining a potential revenue stream and hampering shareholder value.

SHAREHOLDERS EXPECT A RETURN ON IP

Many companies will typically have anywhere from a few dozen to a few thousand U.S. patents. At the high end are industry giants like

IBM or Canon that hold 30,000 to 40,000 patents each in the United States alone. At the other end of the spectrum are start-up companies that, if they are well-funded and well-counseled, might hold a handful of patents or pending patent applications. Either way, portfolios tend to build up over time with little heed paid to how the assets should be deployed. Thus, the portfolio is little more than a hodge-podge collection of disparate patents, with little strategic thought given to why any of the patents exist or how they should be used.

Good patents are expensive assets to simply have sitting around. Patents can take three to four years to obtain, at a cost of between $25,000 and $35,000 each, and post-issuance maintenance fees must be paid (Figure 5.1). Thus, even a small company with a healthy patent portfolio is likely to be sitting on an asset that cost hundreds of thousands, or even millions, of dollars to develop. Not surprisingly, these assets are of great interest to shareholders, who want to know that their money has been well spent and that these assets are being properly deployed. In fact, although there are few reporting requirements for intangibles such as patents, it has been argued that boards of publicly held companies have a fiduciary obligation, perhaps even under Sarbanes-Oxley legislation, to report on the commercial value of IP assets and on the attempts that have been made to obtain value from those assets.[1]

It is very important for a company to take a hard look at its IP assets and determine an action plan for their proper use. These assets could be put to work in many ways—some defensively and some strategically. However, the assets cannot be used until a company knows what it actually has. Thus, the first step toward strategically using a patent portfolio is

---

[1] "Why Directors Must Take Responsibility for Intellectual Property," Robert Greene Sterne and Trevor J. Chaplick," *Intellectual Asset Management,* February/March 2005 Issue #10.

FIGURE 5.1   TYPICAL U.S. PATENT COSTS

Prepare Original Application	$10,000
Response to USPTO Office Action	$ 2,500
USPTO Filing Fees	$ 5,000
Total Cost to Obtain Patent (filing & legal fees)	$17,500
Patent Maintenance Fees (3, 7, 11 yrs)	$ 7,000

The above costs do not include R&D expenditures. Costs are similar or higher (with translations) in other key filing areas, such as Japan.

for a company to organize its patents by aligning its portfolio with its business strategies and objectives. It is surprising how few companies have taken this step, yet it is important because, as business strategies and objectives evolve in response to industry trends, so do the corresponding patent requirements. Patents that may once have been essential can become irrelevant, while new patents may need to be added.

A company engaging in this exercise typically finds its patent portfolio divided into the following three categories:

- **Category A (Need-to-Have):** Core patents needed to execute offensive/defensive business strategies and objectives

- **Category B (Good-to-Have):** Nonessential patents that fall within the company's business, legal, and technical areas of expertise, and thus are candidates for long-term licensing plans

- **Category C (Unrelated):** Nonessential patents that fall outside of the company's areas of expertise, and thus can be sold to generate quick revenue

A company can strategically use to its advantage the patents that fall into categories A (Need-to-Have) and B (Good-to-Have) in several ways. Many of these techniques are explored in detail elsewhere in this

FIGURE 5.2

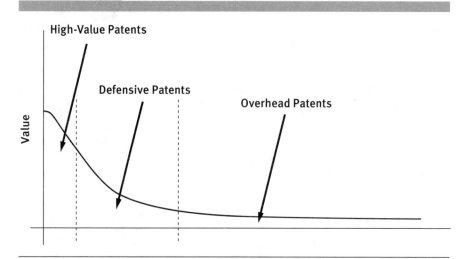

Anatomy of an IT Portfolio. Fewer than 5% of most significant patent port-folios in high-tech have direct value. Some 45% – 50% of patents are neces-sary to maintain for defensive strategy and future growth. But fully 50% or more of patents are unrelated to current activities and serve no productive purpose.

book and won't be belabored here; however, some strategies might be overlooked, to the detriment of the patent holder and shareholder alike (Figure 5.2).

NOT ALL PATENTS ARE CREATED EQUAL

Let's say ACME Technologies has designed and patented its latest widget, and competitor XYZ Systems independently comes up with the same widget. The fact that ACME did it before XYZ and received a patent means that ACME can sue XYZ for infringement. ACME, however, might decide that it can make more money by licensing the patent to XYZ. ACME simply has to decide if the revenue it loses by allowing a competitor into the market is offset by the gain in licensing revenue.

This is the most straightforward way to exploit a patent. Taking it to the next level, assume that ACME Technologies and XYZ Systems have both been in the widget business for a while, and both have patents on their widgets. Of course, widgets are complicated, with lots of moving parts, some of which ACME invented and some that XYZ first invented. One scenario is that the parties can accuse each other of infringement, resulting in a stalemate in which neither company can do business.

This situation is quite common in the IT world. As you might imagine, companies like Hewlett Packard and IBM each have tens of thousands of patents worldwide. These two companies rarely share technology, but each has invented prolifically, each has many patents, and each wants to operate free of claims from the other. The solution for HP and IBM—and for the rival widget makers—is to cross-license, perhaps with a balancing payment. How does it work? IBM might say to HP, "You're using our patents a lot, and we're only using yours a little, so let's give each other cross-licenses, but to balance the value of what we're each getting, you will also pay us $X million." There are many variations on this theme. IBM could license most but not all of its patents, leaving HP unlicensed to some. Or HP could license all its patents but sharply limit which IBM products are licensed to those patents. The key is that at the end of the day, both sides are happy and feel that they received fair value for their IP along with design freedom for their products going forward. Thus, we see one clear benefit of building a patent portfolio: to use as a trading card in a negotiation with another patent holder.

Viewed even more aggressively, a company's ability to enter a market may depend entirely on its patent strategy. Consider the case of Cyrix Corp, which wanted to enter the microprocessor market. Intel has thousands of patents in that area and is known to fiercely defend its inventions against new entrants. Cyrix knew the challenge it faced, so it proactively managed its IP strategy from the beginning to handle this threat. Of course, Intel is many times larger than a tiny start-up like Cyrix, but—as the martial art of ju-jitsu teaches—size can be a disadvantage.

From the outset, Cyrix aggressively sought patents on its new ideas in microprocessor design. At the same time, it made arrangements for an Intel licensee (IBM) to manufacture Cyrix products, as Intel could not claim infringement if the products were made and sold by an Intel licensee. Granted, this arrangement was expensive for Cyrix, but it gave the start-up the breathing room it needed to grow its patent portfolio into a potent weapon it could use against Intel. Here is where Cyrix's smaller size came to be an advantage: because it now had patents to use as trading cards in negotiations with Intel, Cyrix could offer to trade 5% of its revenues for 5% of Intel's revenues. The much bigger Intel wanted no part of such a lopsided financial trade, but it could not rebuff its smaller opponent out of hand. After all, if both sides asserted their patents in court, both could face an injunction. That would hurt Cyrix, but it would be devastating to Intel. Under the circumstances, Intel had no choice but to negotiate a cross-license, which was all Cyrix really wanted. Now it could seek partners other than IBM to manufacture its products—and, generally, be free to function in the marketplace.

Another way a company can utilize patents effectively appears to be paradoxical: not to keep competitors from a course of action, but to encourage them to act in a way that allows the patent holder to sell more products.

Let's say Newco is trying to introduce a new technology. It might be a new modem, or a computer operating system, or a new way to record and play DVDs. In today's interdependent technological eco-system, it's difficult for one company to set such a technology standard. After all, the company that invents a new modem has to ensure that the modem can talk to all kinds of computer operating systems, hardware, phone lines, and so on. Clearly, if the modem is going to have any chance whatsoever, the manufacturer needs to convince the modem ecosystem that its technology is the best. The manufacturer's portfolio of modem industry patents can be powerfully persuasive in this regard. For example, the manufacturer might tell the industry, "Sure, you can go in some other direction with your modems, but you should know that I have a patent on that direction and I'm going to charge a hefty royalty on it. However, if you choose to go in my preferred direction, I won't charge you anything."

This combines two of the techniques we've discussed. The manufacturer has used a patent on an invention it has decided not to bring to fruition to block one technological avenue while offering an attractive cross-licensing opportunity to encourage others to go down the technological avenue it prefers. Similarly, a patent holder can influence its environment by reducing its costs. For example, it's possible that another company, Oldco, manufactures a cog used in Newco's widgets, and that cog infringes on Newco's patents. This scenario occurs frequently. After all, it's highly likely that Newco, with lots of R&D in the area of improved cog use, holds numerous cog-related patents. It could go to Oldco and demand a licensing fee, except for one catch: Newco needs those cogs in its widgets. So instead Newco decides to ask Oldco to knock a nickel off the price of each cog it supplies to it for the next five years. In exchange, Oldco acquires a license that allows it to sell its Z cogs in the general marketplace—but at a higher price to all of Newco's competitors.

Now, let's reverse the above scenario. Newco, the biggest customer for cogs, is infringing on Oldco's patent. What's a cog maker to do? It can't very well go to its biggest customer and say, "You're infringing on my patents, and by the way, how about increasing your order for my cogs?" The cog maker will no longer have a customer; it will have a lawsuit. The cog maker vendor needs to keep its customer, avoid the lawsuit, and still get value for its invention.

One way to achieve this goal is to create a consortium with other cog makers and have that group grant licenses to the patent in question. The cog maker might not directly collect on its customer's infringement, but the cog maker still collects a royalty and keeps the customer. This technique has been employed successfully by members of the MPEG committee and DVD designers. Another approach is for the cog maker to do an end run around the customer by going to the widget consortium and saying, "Right now, many of you are buying cogs from my competitor(s), and thus your widgets are infringing on my cog patents. So, you can either pay me a royalty on the sale of your widgets using my competitor's patent-infringing cogs or buy the cogs directly from me." The cog makers' increased sales will more than make up for lost licensing revenue. In all of these examples so far, the patentee gains revenue by giving up exclusivity on the patents.

But yielding rights doesn't have to be an all-or-nothing deal. A patentee can have its cake and eat it, too. Let's say that Newco has an innovative feature for its computer keyboard—a stick shift in the middle—that does something new, useful, and non-obvious. In short, it meets the preliminary and basic standards necessary to receive a patent. No way is Newco going to license anyone on the patent for this new keyboard feature. It wants the world at large to think of Newco when they think of keyboards with stick shifts. So it tells the other keyboard manufacturers that it will negotiate cross-licenses for all of the other patents in its collection, but no one can have a license to the new stick shift because Newco wants to maintain the technological advantage in the marketplace this innovation provides. The other keyboard manufacturers might say, "We won't license your other keyboard patents unless you include the one covering the stick shift." Or they might say, "Fine, if we can't have the stick shift patent, then you can't have a license to our cool new technology." The back and forth between the manufacturers in this scenario becomes a negotiation, but the point is that a company need not put all of its cards on the table when licensing a patent portfolio. A company can hold back a license to those patents or those technologies that make its products unique.

DEPLOYING UNRELATED OR ORPHAN PATENTS

So far we have explored some of the ways that a company can profit through various licensing techniques, but there's an alternative approach that many companies overlook: that intellectual property, like real property, can be sold. In fact, selling an IP asset is often the best course of action. Unfortunately, IP holders tend to have a knee-jerk reaction to the idea of selling some or all of their patents. They worry that they might be giving up something good, selling too cheaply, or not retaining patents that might later be used against them or their customers. Sometimes the fear of doing the wrong thing leads to doing nothing at all and often culminates in patent abandonment. Companies would not dream of abandoning valuable, but underused assets like real estate or inventory by simply failing to pay their local taxes or rent on the warehouse. However, that is precisely what many U.S. patentees do with startling frequency. In fact, more than 50,000 patents are abandoned annually for failure to pay maintenance fees (Figure 5.3).

That's a shame, because selling unneeded or category C patents can generate income a company can use to:

- **Raise capital**—for a quick return on an asset and to add value to a spin out

- **Save money**—by avoiding maintenance fees

- **Generate income to buy patents**—that the company's evolving business strategy indicates it needs to fill newly evolved holes in its patent portfolio

FIGURE 5.3   TOTAL PATENTS ABANDONED/
MAINTAINED

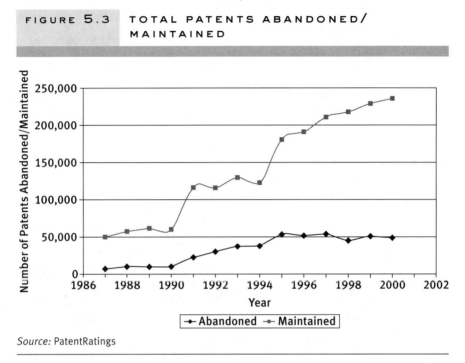

Source: PatentRatings

Hard to Part. Patents are more likely to be maintained in 2000 than in 1990.

- **Recoup filing and preparation costs**—selling old patents can finance the filing of new patents

Regarding the potential problem of a transaction coming back to haunt a seller, the buyer can always negotiate the right to procure a license back to the seller (and the seller's customers) if needed. Take the case of Lockheed, a huge company that's employed a lot of good engineers who have come up with interesting technology. Of course, Lockheed has patent lawyers who apply for patents on the company's varied inventions. Over the years, Lockheed found itself with a very large patent portfolio. Recently, Lockheed decided to take a hard look at its portfolio and separate out those patents that would enhance its business strategy. For example, Lockheed has a large satellite business, so it needed patents that ensured it could differentiate its satellites and get cross-licenses from other satellite makers. But Lockheed also found that it had several C-type "Unrelated" communications patents it garnered when it was exploring different ways to communicate with satellites, including some covering technology used by wireless networks today.

Instead of making the kind of large investment in its category C patents that would be required to license them out, Lockheed instead held the equivalent of a patent yard sale. It put its category C patents out on a metaphorical front lawn with a "for sale" sign on each of them. Sure enough, along came someone who saw a strategic advantage to owning those patents, and a deal was arranged.

WHO ARE THE BUYERS?

Patent buyers are typically companies whose evolving business strategies have revealed weaknesses in their own patent portfolios. A communications company that might have heeded the advice in this chapter about taking a proactive look at its portfolio, discovered that it was vulnerable to an infringement accusation being asserted by one of its competitor's, and needed the Lockheed patents to allow it to do some patent license horse-trading.

Other buyers of Lockheed's unneeded patents might be companies whose core business is essentially building new portfolios of various patents for investment or future resale. These companies are prepared to invest the amount of time and money to build and license such portfolios and materialize their value.

It's not just big companies like Lockheed that are holding these yard sales. Smaller companies, some with just a handful of patents in their portfolio, are making money by holding their five or so core patents and selling the rest. This appeals tremendously to CFOs and General Counsels alike. The former are always looking for ways to cut costs and

will pressure the legal department to keep patent costs flat while still filing for more protection of the company's inventions. This is difficult,
because an ever-growing portfolio requires increased legal expenses. The
solution is to aggressively prune the portfolio and sell off unneeded
assets (after all, what was important two years ago may be a "don't-
care" issue today), using the proceeds to support the strategically important filings.

The process of selling patents can also be mercifully quick—often
just a matter of weeks. That's especially true if what a company has to
sell is a desirable patent that's well written, reads on a hot technology
market, and can be easily used in the manner (e.g., cross-licensing)
outlined earlier. Patents speak for themselves, but being able to show
a prospective buyer how a patent is relevant to a market makes it im-
mensely more attractive. A patent seller can also help quickly put to
rest other due diligence issues by:

- **Making clear what is being sold.** Does the seller have all the
  rights to the patent in terms of joint ownership issues and licenses?
  A company will get a better price if it can show it has all the rights
  to the patent being sold.
- **Making sure all maintenance fees are paid.**
- **Making sure the chain of title is clear and correct.** Have the
  patents been pledged as collateral? Does the Patent Office have
  the correct information on file?
- **Making sure all the parents, children, sibling, and international
  counterparts are included.**

Buying and selling patents is a lot like buying and selling real estate.
As in selling a home, there can be an agent who represents the patent
seller by explaining the technology, contacting prospective buyers, and
taking a percentage of the patent's sale price (typically, 10% to 30%,
but it can be as high as 50%) for his or her services in this regard. There

are also finder agents who work for the buyer and facilitate the process. As when selling a home, a reasonable asking price is important for serious patent sellers. Mutually beneficial patent transactions are frequently stymied by unreasonable seller price expectations. Inventors love their ideas. Or business executives get stars in their eyes from reading about the sums at stake in high-profile IP litigation. What these executives forget are the risks, that patent owners lose cases, too, and that the majority of patents—even good patents—generate no revenue.

A SELLER'S PARADOX

Ironically, a patent seller's paradox comes into play, because a seller's expectations, often, are often higher when the technology is unused than when it has been commercialized. Because the patented device's implementation is all in the future, it's easy for the seller to conjure an image of a 100% market share and revenue curves that resemble a hockey stick. The reality is that many, if not most, patents derive their value not by being the greatest advance since sliced bread, but simply by being part of a patent portfolio. The good news is that a company can realize more revenue than it ever thought possible on its patents if it takes to heart the main points covered in this chapter:

- Patents can serve as a bridge to significant revenue and enhanced business opportunities.

- Publicly held companies should consider their fiduciary obligation and make every attempt to obtain the most value from their IP assets.

- The first step to strategically using a patent portfolio is to take a hard look at the nature of the intellectual assets. A company needs to organize its patents into "Need," "Good-to-Have," and "Unrelated" categories that reflect its business strategies and objectives.

- A company can use all or part of its patent portfolio as a trading card in negotiations (through cross-licensing, etc.).

- IP assets, like real property, can be sold. Sometimes such sales are the best course of action.

- Patent "yard sales" can generate considerable revenue.

- As with the sale of a home, quick and successful IP transactions require setting a fair price. It helps significantly to put to rest as many due diligence questions as possible by anticipating them, and considering the use of an agent who can facilitate the process for a fee.

There is no such thing as a one-size-fits-all patent portfolio. However, all companies that are building an effective ensemble of IP rights should have the same basic thoughts in mind. A smart company will proactively develop its patent portfolio so that it has several patents in the first two categories: "Need-to-Have" and "Good-to-Have." These will allow the company to implement potent and creative negotiation strategies that not only generate revenue but also provide clear advantage in core markets. The inevitable large number of patents remaining in the "Unrelated" group should not be considered failures; with appropriate expectations, they can be readily converted into cash. Many intellectual asset investors are now beginning to understand that by carefully monitoring their portfolio development via close relations between patent lawyers, engineers, and marketing personnel, a company can have a powerful strategic tool at its disposal, as well as a newly discovered revenue source. Senior executives, boards of directors and others responsible for shareholder value, whatever the size of their business, would be well-advised to bear this in mind.

*W*hile Jefferson and Benjamin Franklin
were generally opposed to the awarding of limited
monopolies to inventors, James Madison and
Alexander Hamilton were in favor of providing
inventors with rewards for their inventions.

—A History of the U.S. Patent Office

Risky Business: Overlooking Patents as Financial Assets

BY JAMES E. MALACKOWSKI

Profile: Wunderkind

At 22, Jim Malackowski was involved in his first patent damages case. It was 1985, just three years after the Court of Appeals for the Federal Circuit had been established, and a $1 million award for patent infringement sounded like a boatload of money to the young analyst. He was on his way. Malackowski went on to become one of the leading damages valuation specialists and expert witnesses in the United States. Three years later he founded IPC Group, which, through a financing by a private equity firm, became InteCap and was sold in 2002 to CRA International, at the time the largest IP consulting and valuation firm for valuation and litigation, for more than $140 million.

The Formula car that Jim Malackowski races has a top speed of 180 mph.

The views expressed in this article reflect those of the author and not Ocean Tomo, LLC.

Malackowski was born in Chesterton, Indiana, to a blue-collar family. His father worked in a steel mill. His image of having to borrow his mom's old station wagon, complete with a flower power decal, is a strong memory from his teen years. Upon graduating from Notre Dame with an accounting degree, it was not financially feasible for him to go to law school.

The first year out of college, Malackowski did manage to buy a used Ferrari 308GTSI Spider, which he fixed up and still owns. He has owned a 1990 Porsche Cabriolet, but has since given it up for something more practical to accommodate his high school sweetheart, Kristie, and their two children, ages six and two. He lives with his family in the Stark family mansion in Chicago, most recently owned by Oprah Winfrey's partner, Jeff Jacobs. The home was built in 1925 as a neighbor to residences owned by Armand Hammer and Oscar Mayer. It is over 13,000 square feet with a coach house and art gallery, and has a reflecting pool and sculpture garden. According to *Crain's Chicago Business,* in 1999 it was the city's most expensive residential sale.

"Understanding the market value of IP assets is the essence of earning a return," says Malackowski, a CPA by training. "Lawyers are not necessarily equipped to understand what makes a patent important to a given business or industry, but financial people are."

In 2003, he established ICMB Ocean Tomo, LLC, now a 60-person IP merchant banking firm specializing in understanding and leveraging intellectual property assets. In 2005, Ocean Tomo ran a successful auction in San Francisco for the sale of Commerce One IP assets. It also established with Perot Investments in August 2005 the Ocean Tomo Capital Fund, a $200 million private equity fund to invest in IP-rich companies.

Malackowski, a youthful-looking 42-year-old, is past president of the Licensing Executives Society, trustee of the National Inventors' Hall of Fame, and director of the International Intellectual Property

Institute, an IP think tank. He is competitive in the same fierce way that many investment bankers tend to be, and he is still in love with fast cars. Not only does he like to close deals for clients, but he is a competitive Formula racecar driver and owner. For the last two years he has raced formula cars professionally in the globally televised Star Mazda series, finishing 2005 third in class with an overall team championship. The Ocean Tomo car attains top speeds of 180 miles per hour and can achieve 0 to 60 miles per hour in a mere 2.9 seconds.

"It's a little harder spending the time on racing now that I have a family," he confesses, "but it's something that is in my blood."

The chapter that follows, "Risky Business," focuses on what happens when senior managements and boards of directors fail to understand or overlook IP assets, a surprisingly frequent occurrence, even among technology-rich businesses.

The U.S. economy that once resembled a stable three-legged stool—manufacturing, services, and invention—now has only one leg to stand on. Manufacturing has effectively moved offshore, and services are quickly following suit. Today, only invention and the revenues that it generates remain to support the standard of wealth that we in developed nations have come to enjoy. Intellectual property now dwarfs all assets in value-at-risk. Intangible assets by some estimates now account for more than 75% of a company's market capitalization. A sample of firms represented by the S&P 500 confirms this transition (Figure 6.1).

The Ocean Tomo data, an update of the Brookings Institutions' 2002 study, reflects more than a $3.5 trillion change in value for only 500 companies, all in less than a quarter century. In macroeconomic cycles, this is warp speed. This phenomenon is not limited to one index or class of business, and its effect is permanent. It would be a challenge

FIGURE 6.1   COMPONENTS OF S&P 500 MARKET VALUE

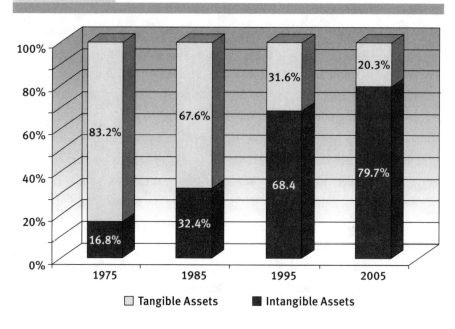

Tangible Assets   ■ Intangible Assets

Source: Brookings Institution, Ocean Tomo

IP Value. Even with a correction for the stock market bubble, 80% of the market value of companies in the S&P 500 are comprised of intangible assets, mostly intellectual property.

for you to identify a larger long-lasting macroeconomic trend in our lifetime. For most readers, the metamorphosis of intangible assets poses an opportunity but also a significant threat. IP is unique and potentially volatile. Managers who fail to treat it with the care and respect it deserves could end up defending not only their business from competitors but also their personal net worth from shareholders. It is essential that companies raise awareness of the value-at-risk inherent within their IP and establish the process and controls necessary to protect their most valuable assets and their officers and directors. My perspective is predicated on more than 20 years in IP finance. Over this time, I have viewed these issues from all sides, including as a consultant, venture-backed principal, venture capitalist, independent director, and trade association president. From my seat, the trends are clearly converging.

Director and Officer Accountability

It is now unacceptable for a senior manager or director to abdicate his or her role in IP management. It is simply too important and too risky to do so. Businesses now face three distinct and potentially viral threats related to intellectual property:

- Patent enforcement litigation
- Sarbanes-Oxley–related compliance
- Shareholder lawsuits

Each of these threats is greater than at any time in history and must be managed from the executive office and boardroom, not the IP counsel's office.

Patent Enforcement Litigation

In the short run, companies are now subject to increasing IP litigation risk, first from competitive peers and then from the growing number of patent "trolls," asserters who make large claims generally with orphan or acquired patents seeking to force a settlement. The number of patent suits in the United States has increased by 152% from 1991 to 2003, according to Brody Berman Associates, Inc. The average time for resolution is slightly more than a year, with a median damages award of $2 million. Awards in excess of $100 million are no longer shocking. Historically, odds have tipped toward the plaintiff, with juries finding in favor of the patent holder 68% of the time compared to 51% in bench trials.[1] Patent enforcement litigation has traditionally been a battle between commercial competitors. Often referred to as the "sport of kings" because of excessive cost, it also embodies curious elements of modern nationalism, where the best offense is often a strong defensive position. A decade ago, it was common that most IP disputes settled with a simple cross-license. Détente is no longer de rigueur.

Today the game and the players are different. Patent enforcement by entrepreneurial investors or agencies is commonplace. Patent trolls have no interest in cross-licensing and seek only maximum financial compensation. Moreover, such enforcement companies are now big businesses, with many reporting collections in excess of several hundreds of millions of dollars. Patent trolls are even going public to raise more capital to acquire more assets to enforce their patents. At least six such firms are actively traded. Look only to Medtronic's recent $1.4 billion patent settlement and acquisition of Karlin Technologies to understand the boundary of financial value at risk. Companies that undermanage their IP assets are subject to increasing litigation risk from their peers. Competitors and former partners who are patent owners may see such companies as takers and not contributors. They will cease coming to them with the idea of exchanging technology in a cross-license and instead approach them with the idea of collecting royalties —a modern version of efficient markets.

Officers and directors must have a plan to manage IP litigation risk, and the plan must be as robust and well articulated as their company's policy for protecting its low-value tangible assets.

---

[1] "The Economics of Patent Litigation," Samson Vermont, p. 327, *From Ideas to Assets,* edited by Bruce Berman, 2002, John Wiley & Sons.

Sarbanes-Oxley–Related Compliance

IP-based regulation is slowly emerging. The good news is that companies have already integrated processes and controls to deal with non-IP compliance issues under the Sarbanes-Oxley Act (SOX). The bad news is that while each of the Fortune 1000 has scores if not hundreds of consultants working on SOX compliance generally, most firms don't have anyone focused on their patents, brands, and trade secrets, even though these assets often are driving the most corporate value. Because the codifying of reporting practices has been among the slowest developments in the IP field, the extent to which this type of reporting will be required is still under development. Although SOX does not specifically refer to IP assets, executives can be sure that some facets of SOX will trigger reporting requirements. Some companies are waiting to see what the requirements will be, but the savvy ones have already started to update their procedures to prepare for what will surely come. If a firm's IP assets have an effect on the company's financial condition and influence investors when they are evaluating the company, they need to be reported and controlled.

Some sophisticated executives are a step ahead. Now, more than ever, all executives need to obtain an in-depth knowledge of the value of their IP portfolios, begin periodic evaluations, learn how new IP is developed and identified, and investigate any claims that have already been brought. Further complicating the matter is that valuing IP is so complex. This means that there are judgment issues involved and a real possibility for manipulation, subjecting IP valuation to a high level of scrutiny. In addition to the government's SOX provisions, other organizations have a keen interest in your IP. The Securities and Exchange Commission (SEC), the American Institute of Certified Public Accountants (AICPA), and the Financial Accounting Standards Board (FASB) are all involved.

Few companies have followed Skandia's lead in the 1990s as an innovator in IP-based reporting; however, a growing number of executives are responding to investor demands and creating new management directives. For example, in the late 1990s, Procter & Gamble decided that it would actively license its IP after three years to anyone who wanted it—including competitors. Today, P&G's IP licensing efforts generate as much profit as a top ten global brand. Likewise, Dow Chemical was an early pioneer in explicitly valuing its IP assets and reporting results internally. Ford Motor created an IP management company, Ford Global Technologies, to focus its IP assets, including their location, for more effective management. And Boeing's IP group appears to grow faster than the size of its aircraft, all to maximize the value of its intangible assets.

Understandably, many companies are reluctant to provide supplementary information that results in potential exposure without delivering a clearly measurable benefit. This attitude will change as reporting organizations introduce guidelines and regulations that pertain to IP. The financial effect of accounting for IP has already been hugely significant. For example, the 2002 introduction of IP-driven FASB regulations, FAS 141 (Business Combinations) and FAS 142 (Goodwill and Other Intangible Assets), resulted in the reported writedown of some $700 billion in goodwill during the year of introduction. Estimates are that corporations will continue to write down $200 billion per year in intangible asset value as a result of FAS 142 alone. Although no new regulations are expected for 2005, part of the solution to IP challenges might be quasi-regulatory solutions that would help companies deal with their ever-increasing IP issues.

A first recommendation would be to explicitly extend the compliance and asset management control issues of SOX to intangible assets. Some would argue that it's already there today, but making the requirements clearer for executives would be a plus. A second recommendation calls for a legal change to balance the risks associated with enforcement by patent trolls, perhaps a decision of the Court of Appeals for the Federal Circuit that effectively holds any firm operating primarily as a technology licensing company potentially liable for inducing infringement of third-party patents when promoting and licensing its technology. Regardless of the current or future regulatory environment, executives need to self-regulate their own companies—to protect themselves, their boards, and their shareholders.

Shareholder Litigation

If a company's competitors, patent trolls, and the regulators do not worry you, its shareholders and lawyers should. In the long run, a company may be subject to IP-based shareholder risk, in part because the near-term enforcement litigation will expose any lack of solid IP management and control. Once such vulnerabilities are exposed, shareholders will hold senior management and directors and, in turn, advisors, accountable for that mismanagement. Companies already operate in a market where an increasing number of class action suits have been filed to compensate shareholders for the mismanagement or undermanagement of intangible assets, as illustrated in Figure 6.2.

Well-established shareholder law firms are beginning to focus on IP as the next great bastion of class action litigation. A typical firm résumé lists its experiences as follows: asbestos, breast implants, tobacco, and now intellectual property litigation. IP is where the action and the money are perceived to be. Who would have believed this even a few years ago? Unmanaged IP is a clear and present danger to almost any company in any industry. The nature of this risk spreads far and wide, (Figure 6.3), as indicated by some of the known patent, brand, and copyright class action matters.

There will surely be more cases, but the upside may be that they will force companies and their executives to ensure that the value of their IP is high relative to the marketplace and managed effectively.

FIGURE 6.2   RECENT IP CLASS ACTION FILINGS

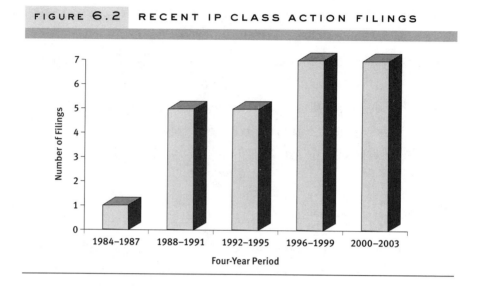

FIGURE 6.3   KNOWN INTELLECTUAL PROPERTY
CLASS ACTIONS

Known Patent Class Actions	Known Brand and Copyright Class Actions
• False assertion of patent coverage	• False press release regarding license to use famous brand
• Failure to disclose adverse facts regarding patent enforcement efforts	• Fraud by holding key brands in CEO name personally (contributed to pattern of racketeering under RICO)
• Failure to disclose inadvertent lapse of key patent maintenance fees	
• False claims regarding licensing agreements	• Failure to disclose in prospectus that company computer products which were derived from IBM products protected by copyright (IBM not a party to suit)
• Promotion of technology known to be not technologically feasible	
• False claims regarding exclusivity of company licences	
• Promotion of known invalid patents	
• Wasting of corporate resources in patent infringement suit without merit	
• False statements in stock prospectus regarding technological capabilities	
• Payment of royalties to inventors after patent expiration	
• Misleading claims in prospectus that company had new patents	

Source: SEC filings

IP-DRIVEN SHAREHOLDER VALUE

Most corporate IP activity and related value are not clearly reflected on reported financial statements. If you look at the balance sheet, in many cases you won't even see intangible assets listed. In the future, it is likely that investors and regulators will seek to unmask these issues. Companies may want to consider doing so voluntarily before they are forced to. Some 90 million Americans depend on the stock market for at least a portion of their retirement income, and there is decreasing tolerance for poor management of assets, including IP assets. Although investors, too, have previously neglected to assess the value of IP in the companies in which they invest, that is no longer the reality. And top companies know they need to get up to speed in evaluating their IP value as quickly as possible.

Some executives are beginning to realize that intangible assets have not only become revenue-producing assets but also have immense potential for significant business growth in the future. Although much more research needs to be done, available quantitative analysis supports the scale of the IP opportunity:

- 80% of the public market value of the S&P 500 is represented by intangible assets
- Over $100 billion annually collected in IP licensing income
- Over $200 billion annually written off from IP impairments
- Over $300 billion annually in unpaid infringements (mostly innocent)
- Only 10% of all technologies are licensed to third parties

Once companies understand the benefits and opportunities of an actively managed IP portfolio, they can use their intangible assets to find new opportunities to generate revenue and capital and become better equipped to confront IP violations of their patents, copyrights, and trademarks. Not only does intellectual property represent one of the largest corporate assets, but history has shown that investment in companies—both large and small—with strong intellectual property outperform all comparable benchmarks. Research confirms that venture capital investments in companies with IP simply perform better. Companies with IP have a significantly greater chance of raising additional capital and half the risk of default.

FIGURE 6.4

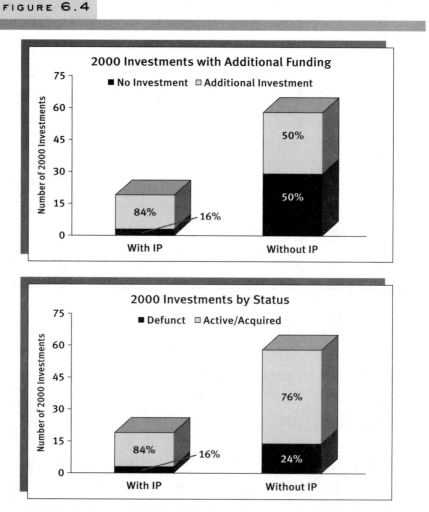

Source: Ocean Tomo, © 2005

The analysis, shown in Figure 6.4, of six leading Silicon Valley venture firms was completed for 1995 and 2002 as well. The results were similar. It is not surprising that the markets are reflecting such high values for certain nontraditional assets. MIT measured it accurately when it shows that the "fortunate 25"—the companies with the highest-quality patents—have been granted the greatest returns by investors. CHI Research, Inc. reported on the leading S&P 500 companies in the *MIT Technology Review,* May 2004 (Figure 6.5).

That's why assigning value to an IP portfolio and actively managing it has to be a top priority. The risks associated with failing to harness the power and potential of IP assets in a timely manner could be even more costly in the long run, translating into loss of competitive advantage and future growth.

FIGURE 6.5

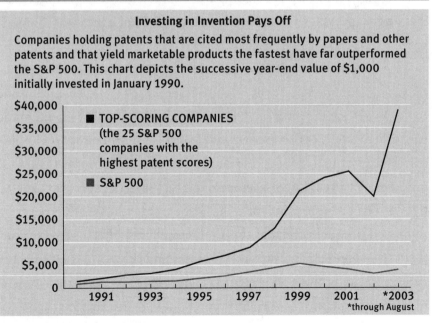

Investing in Invention Pays Off

Companies holding patents that are cited most frequently by papers and other patents and that yield marketable products the fastest have far outperformed the S&P 500. This chart depicts the successive year-end value of $1,000 initially invested in January 1990.

■ TOP-SCORING COMPANIES (the 25 S&P 500 companies with the highest patent scores)

■ S&P 500

*through August

Source: MIT Technology Review

PERFORMANCE MEASUREMENT

One of the foundational tenets of modern management theory is that you cannot manage what you cannot measure (Peter Drucker). However, not all things that should be measured can be measured and, conversely, not all things that can be measured should be measured (Albert Einstein). Conventional IP management tends to focus on what is easily measured—typically, the total number of patents in a portfolio or portfolio segment. This is an all-but-worthless number. (Is it more important for an investor to know how many stocks are in a portfolio manager's fund or which ones?) This focus results in a management process that tends to encourage and proliferate large quantities of patents, without particular regard to the quality, strength, or strategic effectiveness of those patents within specific desired target markets. Simple patent counting makes little sense as a process management metric. Patents are highly unique assets, each having a specific and unique mission in helping accomplish the overall enterprise objectives. The "right" patent can easily be worth the weight of a thousand "wrong" patents.

Licensing revenues are also a popular focus of patent value generation and value measurement (e.g., IBM), but licensing revenues alone typically represent only a small fraction (2% to 3%) of the overall value equation for most corporate-owned patent assets. More important value drivers are (1) maintaining and increasing profit margins on patented products; (2) expanding or leveraging market share; and (3) ensuring freedom of operation and/or reduced risks when navigating new and improved product offerings through densely populated patent minefields. The prevalence of licensing activity and the amount of revenues generated can provide an informative metric for performance benchmarking of an entire portfolio or portfolio segment, and management efforts should obviously focus on this as one measurement of success.

But revenue generation is often not a helpful metric for managing particular patent assets within a portfolio. Most corporate-owned patent assets are valuable for reasons unrelated to licensing. Licensing can also take many years to develop, so there is typically a significant lag period between actual revenues received (the assumed measure of success) and the process being managed (filing and maintenance of specific patent assets). This long lag period results in ineffective management because diagnosis of failure and implementation of remedial course corrections are slow.

Successful patent management actively focuses not on patent counts or pure licensing revenue generation, but on the underlying factors that drive key patent value in the context of the specific mission to be accomplished by each patent and the overall enterprise objectives. Key dashboard metrics we use include, for example, (1) the level of patent protection achieved for a given dollar volume of product sold in each market segment; (2) the number and scope of claims protecting key product features that either drive demand or support premium pricing; (3) the relative crowdedness of the patent space and the rate of patent activity growth/decay; and (4) the level of risk or threat presented by other competitive portfolios in the space.

Some advisors employ sophisticated computer mapping algorithms, statistical regression analysis, and predictive analytics to generate many of the relevant reporting metrics. Statistical models have been developed to objectively rate the quality and value potential of patent assets and entire portfolios based on certain predictor variables (metrics) determined to have statistically significant correlation to patent maintenance rates, maintenance value, and commercialization rates. Also used are several other tools and predictive analytics capabilities that enable us to objectively measure and communicate patent quality and potential value, including time-wise and quality-wise mapping of entire portfolios within a relevant technology space.

DIRECTOR AND OFFICER RESPONSIBILITY

Senior IP management responsibility is absolute but fortunately not complex. Basic steps may be taken to inventory significant IP assets and then risk-manage through appropriate process and control procedures. Tools are now widely available to identify all held patents, allowing them to be analyzed by technology group, International Patent Classification code, and business unit or affiliation. Lists of patents may be prioritized through statistical analysis, ranking scores, and other metrics. For newer technology or nonpatented assets, the process begins by identifying all client patent applications and pending invention disclosures through discussions with R&D staff and appropriate counsel. Joint technical and marketing interviews with business unit leaders are key to identifying likely significant existing trade secrets. Outside vendors can readily determine the status of all trademark registrations and their relevant geographic scope. An efficient review of significant marketing materials can ensure capture of additional potential registrations. Based on analysis similar to this, a listing of personnel reflective of the client's know-how assets can be quickly prepared.

Once an inventory of significant IP is prepared, senior management must turn its attention to issues of process control. For technology, an early requirement is to assess the best method for invention identification and determination of appropriate IP legal protection (or defensive publication). This analysis is not done in a vacuum but rather with the understanding of the interrelationship between corporate strategy, feature implementation, IP protection, and R&D spending. Products ready for market should undergo a program for patent clearance and patent marking. Protocols to protect and escrow corporate trade secrets should be established, and periodic means to assess the need for continued patent maintenance should be in force. A company's legal team should prepare and approve standard form legal contracts associated with

IP, including work-for-hire agreements, purchase orders, employee agreements, and licenses.

Outside of a company's own firm, competitive prudence suggests that you develop a patent landscape of the relevant market showing technology concentration between your offerings and leading competitors. Such analysis allows you to identify significant patent filing trends by competitor by technology. The quality of competitor portfolios may be assessed using similar tools.

Lastly, the licensing and litigation environment should be monitored to evaluate current assertion or licensing efforts and to assess potential litigation risk. Whether it is inventory means for process control, the end result should be to identify IP metrics utilized for reporting purposes.

LOOKING AHEAD

It is more critical than ever for executives to implement a comprehensive approach to ensure better internal management and control of their IP portfolios. Companies must realize that this issue is an executive-level and board-level matter that needs immediate attention. They need to be sure that information flows steadily to board members at every stage. Ideally, someone on the board should be IP-literate to help ensure that the company is properly protecting, reporting, and leveraging its IP. Putting processes into place to ensure that IP is being managed effectively and meeting regulations is a huge task and not one executives should take lightly. Ignorance is no longer an excuse for ignoring intangible value.

... It is quite certain that ever since water has been boiled in covered vessels, men have seen the lids of the vessels rise and fall a little, with a sort of fluttering motion, by force of the steam; but so long as this was not specially observed, and reflected and experimented upon, it came to nothing.

—Abraham Lincoln, 1859

Who Benefits from Patent Enforcement?

BY RAYMOND P. NIRO

"I don't have to be liked by everyone, just respected," Ray Niro once told a reporter.

The founder of Chicago litigation boutique Niro Scavone Haller & Niro has developed a reputation for representing independent inventors and smaller companies in patent lawsuits in which he has an equity stake. To his adversaries, he is often painted as a predator or "troll," or, at least, representing them; to his clients, he is a white knight.

Niro is praised for giving independent inventors and small companies a voice and for helping them to level the playing field. In the high-stakes poker game that is called

It's the high life for litigator, Ray Niro, who tools around in his Ferrari near Independence Pass (elevation 12,095 feet), not far from his Aspen home.

patent litigation, spending $10 million or more on a dispute that goes to trial is not uncommon. Needless to say, Niro, whose firm foots the bill for his time and costs, is selective about the cases he is willing to take on contingency. His team conducts extensive due diligence, which he discusses in the following chapter. He accepts fewer than 20% of the cases his firm reviews.

By any standard, Niro's track record is impressive: more than $500 million won in jury and bench trials and in settlements in more than 200 patent cases over 20 years.

His best-known cases include a $57 million jury verdict in a trade secret suit against a snowmobile manufacturer and its engine supplier, which was later increased to $75.5 million; a $48 million jury award against an ink manufacturer; and a $20 million patent infringement award against Square D Company. In 1997, the *National Law Journal* named him "one of the ten best U.S. litigators," and in 1999 it named him "one of the ten best trial lawyers in Illinois."

Contingency wins, where he might share 40% or more of the recoveries, have made Niro a wealthy man. He lives most of the time in Boca Raton, Florida, and has a home in Aspen, Colorado, which he built with former partner, Gerald Hosier, who is best known for generating more than $1 billion in damages and royalties on behalf of inventor Jerome Lemelson, a known patent submariner until a 1996 change in the patent law to 20 years' exclusivity from filing effectively ended the loophole. (The Lemelson-MIT Program, endowed by the Lemelson Foundation, rewards unsung inventors. MIT describes Lemelson as "one of the world's most prolific inventors.")

Niro loves to go to trial. At 62 years old, the admitted sports fanatic remains fighting fit and lifts weights for 45 minutes four times a week and cycles in Aspen's 8,000-foot altitude. He owns a Falcon 10 jet and at one time owned six Ferraris, including two 360 Spiders and a 575 Maranello. He has 10 grandchildren and has been married to the same woman for 41 years.

The son of an immigrant bricklayer from Abruzzi, Italy, Niro grew up in Pittsburgh, where he says he learned to root for the underdog and still does. Trained as a chemical engineer, Niro is still able to connect with juries and judges. "I learned early on that as a litigator, you need to tell a story that juries and judges understand," he told me. "You can't talk down to anyone. I get great personal satisfaction from helping people to win cases that may not otherwise have been heard."

Frank Calabrese was an underdog. A Waynesboro, Pennsylvania inventor, he claimed his invention, a patented data relay system, was stolen by Square D in the 1980s. He sued when he discovered that the company had been marketing a similar system and refused to pay him for it.

In the four years it took for the case to go to trial, Calabrese developed colon cancer. "Towards the end of the trial," says Niro, "Frank, who was dying, told me 'the money doesn't matter. I want to be vindicated.'" And vindicated he was on January 26, 2000, when a jury awarded Calabrese $13.2 million, which the trial judge later increased to $20 million. Calabrese died 19 days later. "Frank was grateful for what Ray Niro did for him," said Kathleen Calabrese, the inventor's widow. "Ray was the only attorney we could find [who was] willing to take the case on contingency. He worked hard and never gave up on Frank."

But not all of Niro's clients are defenseless little guys. Some are investors, like publicly traded Acacia Technology (NASDAQ: ACTG), which buys patents and asserts them because they understand some companies' aversion to risk and low tolerance for the costs associated with complex patent litigation. To that Niro responds that while he prefers to work directly with inventors and small companies, middlemen can benefit the system and have the right to exist.

Niro's chapter, "Who Benefits from Patent Enforcement?" discusses the importance of asserting patent rights not only for the less resourceful plaintiff but for society as a whole and for innovation.

"When it comes to using patents for business advantage," concludes the bearded litigator, "the little guy is not the one who is gaming the system, although many defendants would like you to think so."

Every economically advanced society has some form of patent system as a means for encouraging innovation and rewarding inventors for their contributions. But a patent is basically worthless if it is not enforced, and enforcement is an expensive business. Many company-owned patents are obtained without any thought of enforcement. They are defensively deployed to discourage competitors from filing lawsuits lest they get sued in retaliation. Other patents are owned by individuals or small companies that often cannot afford the cost or risks of patent litigation, but still see patents as a way to give them a competitive edge.

According to an American Intellectual Property Law Association survey of its members, in 2003, the average cost of a patent infringement suit was between $2 million and $6 million; in Boston, it was $4 million; in New York, $3 million; in Chicago, $3 million; in Los Angeles, $3.5 million. If more than $25 million was at stake, the average cost of litigation soared to between $5 and $5.5 million in New York, Boston, and Chicago and more than $6 million in Los Angeles. Add an additional $400,000 for an appeal and you are well beyond the means of nearly every independent inventor and most small- and medium-sized companies.

On the opposite side of the equation from cost is risk. Economist Gauri Prakash-Canjels of The CapAnalysis Group conducted a comprehensive study of all patent cases that went to final judgment in all federal district courts in the United States between 1990 and 2000.[1] She found that, in 2000, 78% of all the patent cases that went to final judgment (this excludes settlements) resulted in no recovery for the patentee (up from 64% in 1990), and of the 22% that did result in a recovery, roughly half (54%) produced a recovery greater than $1 million. That's one out of ten. If it really costs $2 to $6 million to get

---

[1] "Analysis of Patent Cases," *IDEA: Journal of Law and Technology,* Vol. 41, no. 2 (August 2001).

a 10% chance of recovering more than $1 million, then patent enforcement is not a very good bet.

People are willing to enforce patents for a variety of good reasons. For a competitor that is forced to reduce its market share or lower its pricing because of an infringer, a lawsuit is brought to recapture lost business and collect damages for lost profits and price erosion. For an individual inventor or a company whose business it is to buy and enforce patents, the reason may be to force a license or recover a reasonable royalty. For a company with a rich portfolio of unused patents, it may well have to do with utilizing a dormant corporate asset.

Why then is it so important that patents be enforced? And how can the individual inventor or small company owner afford the costs?

A Patent Is Worthless Without a Remedy

A patent is a Constitutional right that manifests itself in the form of personal property. A patent can be sold, pledged, transferred, or inherited—just like a car or a piece of real estate. A patent's purpose is not simply to provide a technical disclosure of an invention to the public. An article, book, or lecture can accomplish a technical disclosure with considerably less expense. A patent gives its owner the right to exclude others from making, using, or selling the patented invention without the patent owner's permission. This right to exclude—a right with significant costs associated with it—is the key to the patented property. But not all patent rights have value. Some should not have been granted in the first place and may be invalid or unenforceable; others are so narrow they can be avoided easily or are rarely (if ever) infringed.

A patent owner enforces the patent right by bringing a lawsuit for patent infringement in a federal court or by granting a license (a promise not to sue). If a lawsuit for infringement is brought, the remedy can be an injunction preventing further infringement or damages adequate to compensate the patent owner for the infringement that occurred or both. In no event can damages be less than a reasonable royalty, but they can be (and often are) greater. When a license is granted, the consideration is normally a royalty payable over time, generally as a percentage of the net sales price of the otherwise infringing sales. But it can also be a lump-sum amount for a paid-up license, taking into account projections of future sales that might be made through expiration of the patent. Without the right to exclude, however, and without the right to damages, a patent is virtually worthless.

WHEN INVENTORS FAIL, INNOVATION SUFFERS

History has shown that some of the world's greatest inventions were the result of individual inventors working alone in their basements or garages without financial support from either corporations or government. Bob Galvin started Motorola from his garage; the same goes for Steve Wosniak and Steve Jobs, who created the first personal computer. And the Wright Brothers, working from a bicycle shop, never realized their own commercial success with their airplane idea, but they had some good ideas and patented them and, after eight years of litigation that broke their spirit, they were finally successful at least in their enforcement efforts.

As our economy has evolved from one focused on agriculture (19th century) to industry (20th century) to ideas (21st century), it is the ideas, the new inventions, that will drive our economy in the future. Without a strong patent system creating the incentive to invent and a judicial system that allows a reasonable opportunity for inventors (and their investors) to enforce and license their patents, the flow of ideas and the resultant economic benefit will dry up in a hurry.

The Venetians realized this 563 years ago when they passed the Statute of Venice, the first patent law. The Venetians were explorers—world travelers who brought back ideas and recipes from foreign lands—but the chefs of Venice kept their recipes as secrets; when they died, so did their recipes. The solution was to give the chefs the right to use their recipes exclusively (e.g., to practice their inventions) during their lifetime in exchange for the public disclosure of their recipes when they died. As a consequence, the patent system, as we know it today, was born—in exchange for public disclosure of an invention, the inventor is rewarded with a limited monopoly—the right to exclude for a limited period of time.

Famous inventors who create important new businesses are part of the American fabric. Consider the following: Westinghouse (air brake),

SMALL COMPANIES GENERATE JOBS

The inventor of the MRI scanning machine, Dr. Raymond Damadian, was aware of the role small companies play in prosperity:

> Few Americans realize that the great majority of new jobs created for the public are provided by small companies with fewer than 500 employees. From 1981 to 1988, companies with fewer than 500 employees contributed 11.7 million new jobs to the economy. In this period, America's small companies generated two thirds of all new employment.

Ford (car), Gillette (razor), Hewlett-Packard (oscillation generator), Otis (elevator), Harley (motorcycle shock absorber), Colt (revolving gun), Goodrich (tires), Goodyear (synthetic rubber), Carrier (air treatment), Noyce (Intel), Carlson (Xerox), Eastman (laser printer camera), Land (Polaroid), Shockley (semiconductor), Kellogg (grain harvester), DuPont (gun powder), Nobel (explosives), the Wright brothers (aircraft), Owens (glass), Steinway (pianos), Bessemer (steel), Jacuzzi (hot tub), Smith & Wesson (firearms), Burroughs (calculator), Carothers (nylon), Curtiss (aircraft), Houdry (catalytic cracker), Marconi (wireless communication), Goodard (rocket), Diesel (internal combustion engine), Fermi (neutronic reactor), Disney (animation), Sperry (Gyroscope), and Williams (helicopter). Even Abraham Lincoln was granted U.S. Patent No. 6,469 in 1849 for "a device which lifts boats to shoals."

These individuals, in most cases, working alone and without government or corporate support, nevertheless, created not just new inventions, but whole new industries that today employ millions of people.

INVENTORS MUST CONSIDER PATENT ENFORCEMENT

Patent enforcement is expensive, and the results are both risky and uncertain. However, patent owners of all sizes can successfully protect their rights if what they own has value. Failure to enforce a patent that is being infringed squanders the patent asset. Inventors of all sizes and shapes are learning first-hand how painful enforcement can be. The pain occurs frequently because of cost and sometimes because of an honest assessment of risk versus reward. For an individual, enforcement is sometimes the only choice available. Establishing a business against an entrenched competitor may be next to impossible—ditto for the small company. For the larger company, a patent may provide the competitive edge that creates the ability to recover multiples of the research cost for a new product. And large portfolios of patents (like those owned by IBM or Lucent) can become an independent revenue base through licensing.

As noted earlier, one reason that patents must be enforced is that their existence and strength are crucial to our country's economy. Getting a patent is relatively easy, if time consuming. Find an attorney, describe the invention, pay the ever-increasing filing fees, and, if the invention meets the statutory requirements of novelty and nonobviousness and the other criteria (at a cost of $10,000 to $25,000), the patent will issue. The hard part comes after a patent has been issued; things don't get easier for the independent inventor. First, he or she must find a way to make a profit from the invention, either through a company owned by the inventor or by licensing the patent to someone who can commercialize the invention. If the patent is infringed, things just get more difficult, especially for a solo inventor.

Even though invention and litigation are difficult processes for the inventor, infringers must be stopped or made to pay, and this can only be accomplished if inventors enforce their patents. If infringers are allowed to steal inventors' ideas without punishment, the inventive spirit will become extinct and all inventions will eventually become worthless.

Large companies sometimes ignore the ingenuity of the little guy. In one case I had, our client had the good fortune (after a five-year legal battle) of recovering at the time what was the largest collected judgment on a jury verdict in the history of Colorado, more than $75 million. During trial, I showed the jury a document indicating that the defendant believed its options were to negotiate for a license (but that would have been too expensive) or . . . the rest of the document was left blank. The jury understood the second option was to use the invention without paying anything for it.

In Dr. Damadian's case, seven companies infringed his patents on the MRI. In addition to the fact that he was forced to spend years in litigation, Dr. Damadian found that all of the companies—inventor and infringers alike—ended up spending their time and resources in the process of litigation, while they could have been inventing their own products, obtaining their own patents, and building their own new businesses around their new patents, "instead of depending on a business strategy that relies on pirating other people's patents."

PATENT TROLLS AND HARASSMENT

Harassment can be a two-way street. Conferences are now held on the subject of the so-called patent trolls—companies that purchase patents and then seek to license or enforce those patents sometimes against whole industries. Companies that have to defend these efforts claim the system is being abused, that the Constitutional right to promote invention is being undermined, and that legitimate businesses are being unfairly taxed by the cost of investigation and defense and the willingness of some to simply settle for less than the cost of litigation. In June 2005, new patent legislation was introduced in Congress by Representative Lamar Smith of Texas, who said, "I think patent trolls are abusing the system." But who are the trolls? Are they individual inventors, licensing companies, or anyone who has the courage to take on a large corporate infringer?

Larger American companies are learning first-hand through their experiences with China and other emerging countries that, if inventions are not protected, they too will be victimized. According to a September 2004 article in *PC World,* entitled "China Blasted Over Piracy," "a report issued by the Business Software Alliance estimated 92 percent of software used in China during 2003 was unlicensed and illegal." Microsoft has been known to repeatedly bemoan the fact that, in China, a stolen copy of Windows XP can be purchased for around $3. This blatant piracy deprives those who created the idea in the first place of a fair return on the heavy investment they've made to create that idea. As I argued at closing in a case involving Chinese knockoffs of Black & Decker's famous "SnakeLight" flexible flashlight:[2]

> Ask yourselves how much smarter . . . these people must be than
> Black & Decker's engineers, because what took Black & Decker

---

[2] *Black & Decker v. Coleman,* Civil Action Nos. 96-656-A, 96-216-A and 96-1512 (E.D. Va., 8/22/96).

$16 million and 22 months, they were able to do with $126,000 in 8 months.

It's easy to copy. Copiers can sit back and see what is successful, and say, "I will copy that or this." You don't copy failure.

What is the bigger tax on our economy? Copying invention or enforcing patents against infringers? Is a large company the victim of trolling when it is sued for patent infringement, but noble and pure when it enforces its own patents?

If we accept the fact that patents are crucial to a country's economy and that enforcing them is just as crucial, we must deal with the fact that intellectual property litigation is extremely costly, even for large companies. How do we level the playing field? Also, how does a large company that is repeatedly alleged to be infringing patents owned by individuals or patent-holding companies fight back if it feels it really is being victimized by so-called patent trolls?

THE ROLE OF CONTINGENT-FEE REPRESENTATION

Lawyers share the risks of litigation with their clients. For years, lawyers have used contingent-fee representation in the personal injury arena. In fact, 95% of personal injury cases are taken on contingency. That approach has spread to anti-trust litigation, shareholder derivative suits, and, in recent years, to patent litigation.

Deserving inventors and small or underfunded companies with limited resources have a right to their day in court. If it is impossible for them to pay the expense of the litigation, they should not be shut out of the process. Contingent-fee arrangements take two basic forms: (1) a fee based on the result achieved, with the client paying all of the out-of-pocket expenses, or (2) a fee based on the result obtained, with the lawyer advancing all or part of the out-of-pocket expenses. The latter approach is high–risk for the lawyer, because the expenses incurred in most patent cases can be in the range of 25% to 35% of the total expense of the litigation.

THE HIGH COST OF PATENT DISPUTES

Here is the out-of-pocket expense breakdown for a patent infringement case that only went through a one-week trial, but resulted in an eight-figure verdict:

Expert witnesses and consultants	$285,000
LEXIS/Westlaw charges	$ 65,000
Court reporters	$ 40,000
Overnight shipping charges	$ 10,000
Computer consultants	$ 5,000
Legal and support staff overtime	$ 18,000
In-house charges for copies, phone, fax, etc.	$165,000
Outside copying charges	$ 75,000
Court charges and process servers	$ 4,500
Charts and videos	$ 50,000
Travel	$ 45,000
Local counsel	$ 16,000
Miscellaneous	$ 10,000
Total	$788,500

The grand total comes to almost $800,000, and these expenses are modest.

It is one thing to put one's time at risk, but quite another to incur the burden of travel expenses, expert witness fees, court reporter charges, and the like. The latter approach can also encourage some clients to make unreasonable demands on their lawyers to overlitigate or to refuse reasonable settlement offers in hopes of unrealistic results, since they are drawing upon others' capital. On the defense side, it can be argued that the hourly-rate billing system actually encourages long and expensive proceedings. Why leave a stone unturned when one is being paid handsomely to uncover every potential defense, discover every item of alleged prior art, or assert even questionable defenses?

Some lawyers do their contingent-fee cases on a sliding scale: the client pays an increased percentage of the total recoveries, depending on the amount of time expended in the representation. Perhaps 35% of any recoveries obtained before a lawsuit is filed and 40% of any recoveries obtained after a filing of a lawsuit.

What do fee agreements like this accomplish?

- They allow an individual or a small company that owns the patent (each with limited resources) to have access to sound legal representation.

- They keep the judicial system open to everyone, not just those who can afford to spend millions in legal fees.

- They allow small- and medium-sized companies to participate in the process.

- They force patent owners and the lawyers representing them to evaluate the strengths and weaknesses of their cases carefully before filing suit. No one wins by litigating marginal cases on a contingent-fee basis.

- They allow large corporations to enforce their portfolio of patents more aggressively by making patent enforcement more palatable to business managers by capping their litigation budget. It is extremely difficult, if not impossible, to estimate litigation expenses in a patent case (at the outset of the case) with any degree of precision. Business managers, who ultimately pay for the litigation, do not like to be surprised with cost overruns. After all, they are expected to meet their projections on a quarterly or annual basis.

- Finally, contingent-fee agreements require lawyers to be accountable to their clients based on the result achieved. I feel that if more lawyers representing well-financed defendants had to evaluate their cases on what they would be paid based on the result achieved, there might be more early settlements and less of the "scorched earth" litigation tactics we see so often.

LARGE PATENTEES ARE FIGHTING BACK

Some law firms are soliciting clients who are being threatened or sued by the so-called patent trolls. They paint the accused infringers as victims who have to band together to fight the evil inventor who, "heaven forbid," is being represented by contingent-fee lawyers. "Let's pool our resources and fight them, of course, hiring us on an hourly-rate basis." Here's an example of a website solicitation:

> Evaluating a threatened patent portfolio can be quite complex. The effort can be time-consuming, expensive, and unsure in its results. Some "patent terrorists," who are not business competitors and do not seek injunctions, but instead only seek license fees, are quite adept at offering license settlements in lieu of litigation, for one-time up-front cash payments that make the license look cheaper and more secure than litigation.

Part of the game play is to create an image of wild-eyed "terrorists" and the implication of "weakness" if a potential licensee accepts a fair license. Some large companies that feel they are vulnerable are falling for this scare tactic and are sometimes actually combining to act as a group.

Breaking from the Pack

The first challenge for a patentee is to get a potential licensee to think and act independently of the group. In one case, we offered an incentive-ladened deal to the first patentee to sign. Ideas:

- The first one out gets the best deal.

- The last one out pays the most.

- Make deals that say the first to settle pays only 50% of what other parties will pay in the future.

- Rebate royalties to early licensees as new ones sign on.

The defense specialists are also telling their clients that they won't get a better deal by settling early. Nonsense. Challenges to the patent may force later settlements lower, but rarely do licensees get better deals after a lawsuit gets past the summary judgment stage. And if the patentee wins at trial, forget about favorable deals.

Dispelling the Troll Myth

Criminal defense lawyers learned long ago that if you paint the victim as a bad person, the jury might believe the real victim is the defendant. Famous criminal defense lawyer Percy Foreman allegedly said that when he finished trying a murder case the jury felt the victim really deserved to die. Things are not that bad yet in the patent field, but they are getting there. The victims are those poor multibillion-dollar corporations, which were often built on the strength of the patent system. The so-called evil ones are inventors seeking to exploit their patents with the help of lawyers who are willing to take a case on a contingent-fee basis. On the other hand, as Bruce Berman has pointed out in his "IP Investor" column in *IAM* magazine, "despite spending billions in research and development and tens of millions in legal fees for a stockpile of patents, many companies with large patent portfolios are still vulnerable to patent enforcement," particularly if they cannot counterclaim against a nonmanufacturing plaintiff.

An Intel executive coined the term "patent trolls" because his company was sued for defamation for calling one of my clients a "patent extortionist." Since leaving Intel to participate in a patent acquisition group funded by large companies, he has softened his language. To a large company, a so-called patent troll is a taxing body that forces the company to pay "unjust" amounts by threatening or filing frivolous lawsuits. Is the accumulation of hundreds or thousands of patents, which are then offered to investors or potential licensees, "trolling"? It seems there is a fine line between a company that buys five patents to license and, if necessary, enforce, and one that generates hundreds or thousands based on its own R&D. The owner of the large patent portfolio simply has more leverage and possibly can extract a higher toll in a less obvious way. The patent trolling debate has focused light on several key issues.

THE DANGER OF NOT ENFORCING

There are two results associated with failure to enforce good patents: (1) inventors who can't enforce their patents because of the cost or the inability to get someone to represent them simply stop inventing, and their ideas are lost; and (2) the law of the jungle takes over—only the strong (or in this case, the rich) survive. An inventor with a good patent has no chance to build a successful business or obtain a reasonable reward for his or her invention. A good patent has meaning only when a jury, a judge, and a court of appeals say it does.

The methodology for conducting due diligence before filing a lawsuit is clearly defined: hire experts, investigate infringement, get the opponents' views, and litigate across the table if you can. But few things in life are certain, and patent litigation is less certain than most things. Our firm certainly is not "trolling" for random patents to assert. We don't have to. Instead, we have three full-time technical experts who devote their time to helping us investigate new potential cases and decide whether or not we take them. In the end, we reject far more than we take on. When we evaluate a potential case, it is not uncommon for three or more lawyers and two technical experts to invest 100 to 200 hours of their time before representation is accepted and 100 to 200 additional hours before a lawsuit is filed.

LEVELING THE FIELD

We must find ways to level the playing field so individual inventors and smaller, less well-armed companies can enforce their patents, creating an incentive to invent. This is more easily said than done. If patents are worthless unless they are enforced, then there have to be ways to reduce the cost of litigation or encourage lawyers to share the risk and expense with their clients. Otherwise, the incentive to invent is lost. As for the "victim" mentality of some big companies that are being sued or repeatedly threatened by individual inventors or licensing companies, that is just part of the price of doing business. Cases that truly lack merit will be lost, and losing cases or bringing marginal ones creates no economic incentive for contingent-fee lawyers. Responsible lawyers investigate their cases thoroughly before bringing them, often with independent technical experts and a significant investment of lawyer time. Irresponsible lawyers, in time, will disappear because the economics of taking and losing patent cases will drive them out of business, maybe returning the whole idea of trolls to its mythical beginnings.

Alexander Hamilton drafted a competing patent bill [to Jefferson's] that was introduced on March 1, 1792. This bill addressed the issues of handling cases in which disputes regarding overlapping patents were handled.

Hamilton proposed that the Supreme Court of the United States settle such arguments. Additionally, he inserted a provision that allotted the revenue from patent fees to be allocated for the purchasing of books and other scientific apparatus as well as for the establishment of a national library.

—A History of the U.S. Patent Office

Global IP in Crisis:
The Threat to Shareholder Value

BY BRUCE A. LEHMAN

Profile: All Along the Watchtower

On New Year's Eve 1999, Bruce Lehman was ringing in the new millennium in style. At the invitation of Jay Walker, CEO of Priceline.com, he was attending a gala party at Windows on the World atop New York's World Trade Center. At the time, Walker, recently arrived on the *Forbes* 400 richest list, had asked Lehman to join him in establishing new companies on the digital frontier.

"We were all feeling pretty good about the future," recalls Lehman. "Little did we realize that some 20 months later the tech bubble would have burst and the building underneath us would be gone. It was really quite sobering."

Hon. Bruce Lehman conferring with a foreign delegation by a portrait of William Thornton, first Superintendent of Patents. Thornton, who succeeded Thomas Jefferson in this role, is most famous as the architect of the United States Capitol Building.

Lehman, the longest-sitting Commissioner of the United States Patent and Trademark Office (USPTO), served from mid-1993 to almost 1999. He was the first "activist" USPTO head and a principal author of the Digital Millennium Copyright Act (DMCA), which after turbulent negotiations, was approved by the Clinton administration in 1998. Among other things, the Act addresses the use of software and copyrightable material on the Internet.

"Most USPTO Commissioners get through their tenure with few people aware there's even been a change," says Lehman. "I found the job really challenging. We had 7,000 employees and a budget of over $1 billion. It was as much like running an old economy corporation as a government agency."

President Clinton and his advisors were interested in the future of technology, and Lehman was invited to the White House at least monthly for briefings. When he joined the USPTO, Lehman engaged in streamlining the agency to be more responsive and customer-focused. His efforts were recognized by Vice President Gore's National Performance Review as a success story for government reinvention.

In his more than 30 years in Washington, D.C. as an attorney, advisor to Presidents and CEOs, and Under Secretary of Commerce, Lehman has observed first-hand the power of IP rights. "Washington is a little bit like Hollywood or Silicon Valley," he says. "It's a company town with A, B, and C players. You need to be on good enough terms with all sides of the political spectrum, as well as with your allies."

Born in Beloit, Wisconsin, Lehman's father died when he was 13, and his mother went to work in a bank to support him and his sister. "Growing up without much money in the Midwest taught me about democratic values and helping people as a part of everyday family life," he recalls.

To maintain USPTO initiatives begun under his administration, Lehman founded in 1999 the International Intellectual Property Institute (www.iipi.org), a nonpartisan, nonprofit IP development organization and think tank that assists developing nations and patent offices and examines IP issues. He divides his time between service as chairman of the IIPI and being of counsel to Akin Gump Straus Hauer & Feld, the international law firm.

Lehman, 60 years old, is as well informed as any IP advisor in Washington. A student of history, Lehman speaks serviceable French and enjoys foreign travel, where his post as policy advisor to the Director General of the World Intellectual Property Organization (WIPO), the specialized United Nations agency headquartered in Geneva, often takes him. A frequent speaker, he enjoys discussing politics as much as patent rights. Lehman is at ease in diverse cultural settings, and is on a first-name basis with almost everyone important in domestic and international IP, including current and past heads of the EPO, JPO, WIPO, the China PTO, and the USPTO. He prides himself on being the foremost authority on patent offices and procedures worldwide, but he can be impatient with mediocrity and provincial thinking.

"People who know Bruce tend to feel strongly about him," notes a colleague. "He is not a 'yes' man. He feels so passionately about his positions that he sometimes wears them on his sleeve. But no one can accuse him of not being informed about the issues or being insincere about the importance of IP rights."

In 1994, the *National Law Journal*, the largest-selling legal weekly, named Lehman its "Lawyer of the Year." In 1997, another publication, the *National Journal,* a Washington-based national magazine of public policy, named him one of the 100 most influential men and women in Washington. Lehman was the first openly gay male to be confirmed by the U.S. Congress.

For 10 years before joining the Clinton administration, he was a partner in the Washington, D.C. law firm of Swidler & Berlin. There he represented individuals, companies, and trade associations in the areas of intellectual property rights. His clients were drawn from the motion picture, telecommunications, pharmaceutical, computer software, and broadcasting industries.

Prior to entering private practice, Lehman worked for nine years in the U.S. House of Representatives as counsel to the Committee on the Judiciary and chief counsel to the Subcommittee on Courts, Civil Liberties, and the Administration of Justice. Lehman was the Committee's principal legal advisor in the drafting of the 1976 Copyright Act, the 1980 Computer Software Amendments, and 1982 Amendments to the Patent Laws.

Patent uncertainty and costs are of vital concern to Lehman. He believes that equipping patent offices with the tools necessary to do the job and companies and inventors with the knowledge of how the system works are keys to the future. In the following chapter, he ponders what has to happen to remove the lethal combination of poorly issued patents, unpredictable courts and skyrocketing damages.

Most senior managements don't have a clue how profoundly intellectual property rights affect their bottom line. While generating a return on all assets is their primary responsibility, they lack perspective about the role patents and other IP play in generating profit, maintaining market share, and creating value. They are also uninformed about the impact on results of global IP policy, especially in developing nations like China and India.

Understanding IP assets, which represent as much as 90% of the market value of some companies, remains a dangerously black art. An inefficient IP system, such as the one that currently exists, costs shareholders and consumers everywhere, and is a potential threat to innovation. Executives and boards who believe that shaping global IP policy can be delegated to their lieutenants and attorneys, like a messy technology dispute, may soon find themselves, and their companies, left out in the cold.

Patent quality is a concern for companies of all sizes and types. No longer does a large patent portfolio insulate a company from local "trolls" who are out for an easy buck or from international predators. Companies in some industries are more IP-dependent than others. Virtually all of the value of innovative pharmaceutical, chemical, and biotech companies lies in their patents. This is also true for companies broadly defined as information technology, such as those in computer hardware, components, and telecommunications. For media and software companies, value frequently lies in their portfolio of copyrights.

Given the market advantage afforded by certain intellectual property rights, it is surprising that so few CEOs give personal attention to key developments that lie at the heart of what has become a global intellectual property system. These developments have a direct influence on corporate value, and I fear that abdicating their oversight to those without the sufficient vision or decision-making authority is a proverbial accident waiting to happen.

THE LEADERSHIP VACUUM

During 30-plus years in Washington, D.C., I have witnessed this leadership failure first-hand, in my role as Chief Counsel to the Congressional IP subcommittee, a lawyer in private practice, and as Commissioner of Patents and Trademarks in the Clinton administration. All too often, when CEOs visit Congress, Cabinet offices, and the White House, they are more eager to discuss tax policy, environmental law—or even immigration policy—than the national and global infrastructure that protects their companies' patents, copyrights, and trademarks. Usually, discussions about intellectual property issues are left to "green-eye-shade" lawyers from the corporate law department or to midlevel Washington lobbyists. This sends the message to global and Washington decision makers that IP issues aren't really that important, and leads to the kind of broad weakening of the IP system that we are now experiencing.

THE TOP U.S. PATENTEES ARE NOT U.S. COMPANIES

Thirteen of the top 20 companies awarded patents by the U.S. Patent and Trademark Office in 2004 are companies whose primary business is based outside of the United States (Figure 8.1). Companies based in China, India, and other nations are likely to be added to this list by 2020. Without a viable system to issue and uphold patents in other

FIGURE 8.1   U.S. PATENTS ISSUED—2004

Rank	Name	U.S. Patents Issued in 2004
1	International Business Machines Corp	3,277
2	**Matsushita Electric Industrial Co Ltd JP**	**1,965**
3	**Canon K K JP**	**1,813**
4	Hewlett-Packard Development Co L P	1,761
4	Micron Technology Inc.	1,761
6	**Samsung Electronics Co Ltd KR**	**1,605**
7	Intel Corp	1,604
8	**Hitachi Ltd JP**	**1,533**
9	**Sony Corp JP**	**1,348**
10	**Toshiba Corp JP**	**1,343**
11	**Fujitsu Ltd JP**	**1,320**
12	**Koniklijke Philips Electronics N V NL**	**1,224**
13	**Fuji Photo Film Co Ltd JP**	**1,030**
14	General Electric Co	978
15	**Renesas Technology Corp JP**	**917**
16	Texas Instruments Inc	915
17	**Bosch, Robert GmbH DE**	**907**
18	**Seiko Epson Corp JP**	**858**
19	**NEC Corp JP**	**826**
20	Advanced Micro Devices Inc	803

*Bolded names denote foreign companies.   *Source:* IFI Claims

Chart: Brody Berman Associates

Asian nations, U.S. patent and other IP protections are in danger of being eroded.

While the 1990s was a time of strengthening of the global intellectual property systems, recent years have seen a dangerous shift toward weakening IP protections around the world. The thought is that those with patents have too much power or that the patent system is somehow broken and in need of a major overhaul. For example, in the current Doha Round of trade negotiations, developing countries are pressing for lowering the high level of IP protection reflected in the TRIPS Agreement (Trade-Related Aspects of Intellectual Property Rights) that was achieved in 1994 in the prior Uruguay Round of trade discussions. An illustration of this pressure for weaker IP rights is a proposal by Brazil and 13 other developing countries to modify the charter of the World Intellectual Property Organization (WIPO) to establish the principle that a country's level of intellectual property rights should reflect its level of development. In other words, the poorer the country, the less it needs to recognize and enforce intellectual property rights. While this approach may seem fair to some, it is potentially very dangerous to innovation and world prosperity, not to mention shareholder value.

Another problem that has surfaced in WIPO concerns negotiations to harmonize the world's patent laws. For several years, WIPO has been attempting to formulate a new patent law treaty. For the most part, negotiators from the United States and other developed countries have been experts from national patent offices, who are genuinely seeking to reach agreement on important technical and legal issues (e.g., prior art, grace period, novelty, and inventive step) to improve the efficiency and operation of national and regional patent systems. In contrast, the representatives from developing countries are largely trade diplomats who also deal with highly political trade issues. Rather than improving the coordination and functioning of national and regional patent offices, their goal is to extract concessions on trade issues. In addition, they actively work to stall progress on the technical and legal IP issues of interest to examining offices in an effort to gain leverage in trade negotiations that are taking place in WIPO's sister organization, WTO.

Another disturbing development is the number of anti-IP non-governmental organizations attending WIPO meetings. Examples are The Consumer Project on Technology—an anti-patent organization connected with activist Ralph Nader and Doctors Without Borders, an international AIDS organization that opposes patent protection for medicines in developing countries. Their aggressive presence and lobbying at WIPO are making it more difficult to harmonize and strengthen the patent system. By contrast, there has been much more limited and ineffective participation by IP-dependent industries in WIPO.

Ironically, while the financial press is full of stories emphasizing the importance of global markets and developing economies to corporate growth, few corporate leaders today seem to be responding to these assaults on the system that protects their shareholders' intellectual property rights in these very same markets. If this assault on the international IP system is to be controlled, senior management of IP-dependent companies (practically every global 1,000 company) need to become more engaged, proactively working with their own governments and sending the message that strong IP protection and enforcement is worth fighting for.

THE DANGERS OF UNCERTAINTY

Lack of effective harmonization means that it is exceedingly cumbersome, expensive, and redundant to file for and obtain patent protection, not only in emerging developing countries like China and Brazil, but even in developed countries like the United States and Japan. Today, a patent application from a multinational company is examined from scratch in each country in which it is filed. This means that Japanese, American, and European patent examiners are duplicating one another's work. This not only increases the cost of international patent filings, but the workload created by redundant examination also unnecessarily strains the resources of individual patent offices and leads to longer pendency for all applicants.

An example is the USPTO, where the strain of duplicating work already done in other big patent offices could lead to nearly 1.5 million unexamined applications if remedial action is not taken soon. In addition, the strain on the big national patent offices can lead to poorly examined patents that are more likely to be subject to litigation after they are issued. This greatly increases the cost of doing business for a technology company. Legal fees for the average patent trial in the United States today typically range from $4 million to $10 million and more.

Then there is the uncertainty both for patent applicants and their competitors of not knowing the extent of patent claims for increasingly long periods or how the courts are likely to treat disputed patents. In the United States, the average pendency of applications currently is 20.2 months to a first office action and 30 months to allowance. In many of the critical, newer technologies, current pendency is much longer. Without any relief, the number of unexamined patent applications will rise from the current level of 457,000 to 1,489,000 by 2010. This will mean an average of 36 months to first office action and 43 months to allowance, with no end in sight. This will result in an unhealthy marketplace for innovation-centric companies and their shareholders.

VIAGRA® IN CHINA

The uncertainty created by long pendency, unpredictable courts and questionable examination quality in the USPTO and other developed country patent offices is only part of the larger crisis in the international intellectual property system. Equally important is the often inadequate and sometimes highly political administration of patent rights in big but still developing countries. China's handling of patents on highly successful pharmaceutical products is one example, notably with regard to Pfizer's rights to its blockbuster Viagra product (2004 sales, $1.7 billion).

Pfizer applied for a patent on Viagra in China, and the patent was issued in 2001. It then began a marketing program in that country. However, in 2004, China's State Intellectual Property Office overturned the patent for Sildenafil citrate, the active ingredient in Viagra, in response to a challenge from local generic manufacturers. According to Pfizer, the patent on Viagra was overturned (by China) on the grounds that certain laboratory data was not included in the original patent application. But, Pfizer asserts that at the time of filing there was no requirement for such data.[1]

Pfizer is not the only pharmaceutical company to have its patent revoked in China. In August 2003, Glaxo SmithKline abandoned its patent for the diabetes treatment rosiglitazone maleate (Avandia®) after it was challenged by four Chinese generic manufacturers.[2]

These two cases of revocation by the State Intellectual Property Office are a vivid illustration of the inadequacy of the existing system of country-by-country patent examination when a multinational company attempts to recoup its research costs through sales in emerging developing country markets with immature patent systems. The problems faced by pharmaceutical companies in China are examples of

---

[1] In-Pharma Technologist.com, *Drug Industry Concern as China Breaks Viagra Patent*, found at www.in-pharmatechnologist.com/news/news-ng.asp?n=53413-drug-industry-concern.

[2] *Howard, Patent Finds Rumble in China*, news@nature.com, found at www.nature.com/news/2004/041129/pf/nrd1595_pf.html.

the negative effects of an archaic international system of country-by-country patent examination in important emerging markets that either lack competent patent authorities and judicial systems, or where bureaucrats can be pressured by domestic industries.

Pharmaceutical patents in countries other than China are under attack as some governments threaten to use health emergencies to justify compulsory licensing of patented medicines, particularly antiretrovirals used in the treatment of HIV disease. While in some very poor countries—especially in Africa—there cannot be a meaningful commercial market for high-end patented pharmaceuticals, this is not true in many midlevel and growing developing countries. As this book is being written, Brazil is threatening to revoke Abbott's patent rights to its popular Keletra® HIV therapy unless the company agrees to vastly reduced prices for its product. Brazil only has 150,000 AIDS patients and can easily afford to pay the market price for these products. Unfortunately, it is using its administration of the patent system to threaten Abbott's ability to earn a reasonable return on its investment in that country.

This kind of parochial and short-sighted patent policy does not serve the long-term interests of emerging developing countries. Countries like China and Brazil have their own emergent technology industries, and these industries will not be able to draw investment, grow, and be able to protect their own patents in foreign jurisdictions unless the international patent system is improved, made less costly, and freed of parochial political influences.

AN ACTION PLAN

Solutions to the crisis in the global patent system are more political than costly. They include conserving resources and increasing examination quality by reducing duplication of examinations, sharing work among national patent offices, harmonizing international examination, and, ultimately, creating a multinational PTO in the Asia–Pacific region similar to the European Patent Office.

Duplicate filings in multiple countries account overwhelmingly for the huge increase in total filings. While most applicants file and complete the patent application process in only a select number of the 128 member states of the Patent Cooperation Treaty, it is increasingly imperative to file in a large number of them, particularly in the emerging markets that are a part of APEC. Although one-stop filing and examination is possible for the 28 member states of the European Patent Office, there is no counterpart to eliminate costly and duplicative examination in the Asia–Pacific region, economically, the fastest growing region in the world.

The number of patent offices capable of effectively searching and examining in all fields of technology is very small. There are only 10 patent offices in the world that qualify as international searching authorities and international preliminary examining authorities under articles 16 and 32 of the Patent Cooperation Treaty, and most of these offices lack comprehensive capability to examine in all technologies.

Much of the stress on the international system could be relieved by concentrating examination in a few regional patent offices along the model of the EPO. Short of that, a system of work sharing of the kind embodied in the system of Modified Substantive Examination (MSE) used in Australia, Malaysia, Singapore, and Croatia would eliminate much of the duplication of work in national offices examining the same patent application. Under the MSE system, there is a simplified examination following submission by an applicant of the results of the work of another country's patent office.

The big three patent offices of the world, the USPTO, the EPO, and the JPO, are currently experimenting with the kind of work sharing that could eliminate much of the duplication involved in processing

multinational applications. However, for this system to provide significant relief to the USPTO—the most stressed of the big three offices
—arrangements must be made to provide the USPTO with search
and examination reports from its sister offices far earlier than is the
case today. Both the JPO and the EPO have systems of deferred examination. Many Japanese applicants elect to defer examination for up
to 36 months before any work is done on the application. The result is
that, even with its current high pendency rate, the USPTO completes
examination of Japanese origin patents before the commencement
of examination in Japan. If Japan were to provide more timely examination results to the USPTO and the USPTO were to conduct a
simplified examination based on those results, the caseload of full
examination at the USPTO would drop by as much as 50,000 applications per year, taking a huge amount of pressure off the U.S. office.

The ultimate solution to the patent crisis in the Asia-Pacific region
as well as in the United States would be the creation of an Asia-Pacific
Patent Office similar to the European Patent Office. Like the EPO,
the creation of this office would not require the abolition of existing national offices. Rather, it would offer a one-stop alternative to
country-by-country examination that would be far more efficient
and provide better-quality examinations at less cost than is currently
the case in the region. For all practical purposes, it would reduce filings to two regional offices: the EPO for the expanded European
Union and the Asia-Pacific Office for the Americas, the Pacific, and
Asia—especially if two non-APEC countries, Brazil and India, eventually could be brought in as well. Courts would remain national. In
addition to lower costs and efficiency, a regional patent office would
have an inherently harmonizing effect on international patent law.
The existence of the EPO has had such an effect in Europe by bringing new subject matter—biotechnology and software—within the
European system. The EPO's Expanded Board of Appeals has created

a patent jurisprudence that has harmonized patent law throughout Europe.

The first step in any effort to resolve the global patent crisis should be energizing existing efforts of the national offices, particularly those involving substantive harmonization and work sharing. Japan and the United States could cooperate in leading this effort. Accelerated government-to-government discussions could take place on a bilateral and regional basis, with a focus on APEC. APEC's Intellectual Property Experts Group should be commissioned to develop a concrete plan to address the patent crisis in the region. This plan should focus on implementing substantive harmonization within the region as soon as possible. Concurrently, efforts to share work among willing patent offices in the region should be put on a fast track. In the case of the United States and Japan, this will take the form of encouraging Japan to provide search and examination results for Japanese origin patents much earlier than is the case presently. Patent-dependent Japanese industries need to provide political support to the JPO to the extent that such a change may require the approval of the Japanese Diet.

To the extent that smaller, but sophisticated offices such as those in Canada and Australia can develop specialized areas of competence, similar arrangements might be made with the USPTO and others wishing to avoid duplication of effort. This will lead to a more harmonized regional system and reduced pendency, particularly in the USPTO. In the case of other countries in the region, accelerated efforts will be made to encourage the use of modified substantive examination of the kind currently utilized by Australia, Malaysia, and Singapore.

In addition, the USPTO needs to accelerate solutions to the patent crisis already in the planning stages and to develop new solutions. This should include greater collaboration with industry in areas such as digital file management and searching as well as improving electronic access to relevant prior art. To the extent that the USPTO experiences difficulties in implementing solutions because of uncooperative union leadership, it needs stronger industry support for the USPTO's position.

MANAGEMENTS NEED TO STEP UP

Bob Dylan once said that "you don't need a weathervane to know which way the wind blows." At the same time as the short-term solutions described in the previous section are put into place, the industry needs to work more aggressively with governments in the Asia-Pacific region to design and create an Asia-Pacific Patent Office that will provide to all nations in the region a harmonized multinational examination of the kind now available through the EPO for its member states. This will benefit all nations, regardless of their immediate self-interest, and provide a consistent and globally recognized system of rights that will save money and promote innovation.

None of the urgently needed reforms will take place without stronger leadership from the private sector. Meaningful reform cannot be left to busy lawyers working part-time though bar association committees or middle managers. Policy makers need to know that preservation of the global IP system is a matter of tremendous importance to industry and shareholders at the highest levels. If CEOs of major companies, with the help of IP strategists, learn to understand the issues and take a personal interest in IP rights and actively support a meaningful international patent system, a handful of developing country diplomats and self-proclaimed activists will find it difficult to undermine some of our most valuable resources. A compromised patent system results not only in lower IP standards and more costly disputes, but is also a drain on shareholder value and precious R&D resources, and impedes innovation. The good news is that early and proactive intervention can nip it in the bud.

To promote the progress of science and useful arts, by securing for limited times to authors and inventors the right to their respective writings and discoveries.

High Regard

The Founding Fathers held in high regard the power for Congress to promote science and the useful arts. The following are among the laws that immediately follow establishment of limited exclusivity for authors and inventors provided in Article I, Section 8, Clause 8 of The United States Constitution:

- To coin money

- To declare war

- To raise and support armies

- To provide for calling forth the militia to execute the laws of the union, suppress insurrections and repel invasions

—The United States Constitution, 1787

CHAPTER 9

It Takes More Than Being Right to Win a Patent Dispute

BY RONALD J. SCHUTZ

Profile: Serious Competitor

Ron Schutz enjoys a good fight. The veteran of three triathlons and longtime Minnesota resident will train in just about any weather. "I'm usually good running down to about 10 below zero, Fahrenheit" he says. "I need all the stamina I can get for trial work."

Schutz is a tough competitor. He is directly responsible for intellectual property damages awards and settlements in excess of $350 million. In 1995, he represented Fonar Corporation in a case against General Electric involving infringement of its patent for producing multiple magnetic resonance imaging (MRI) images at different angles during a single scan. The jury in New York awarded his client $110.5 million. The case was affirmed on appeal in the amount of $103 million and was cited at the time in *Intellectual Property Worldwide*

Don't mess with triathlete Ron Schutz. He has won more than $400 million in recoveries for IP clients.

as "the largest patent jury verdict ever upheld." The final award with interest was $128 million.

Schutz learned how to litigate in the Army, where he served four years in the Judge Advocate General's (JAG) Corps. He tried some 20 felony jury trials, including those for murder, rape, kidnapping, and embezzlement.

When he finished his stint with the JAG Corps, he figured that patent litigation would be a good use of his diverse trial skills and engineering education. "This was shortly after the creation of the CAFC [Court of Appeals for the Federal Circuit in Washington]," Schutz recalls, "and just as renewed interest in patents was about to take place."

What sets Schutz apart from other patent attorneys is his ability to translate complex technical information into the language that a jury can understand, at the same time weaving it into a compelling story. The manner of a humble Midwestern lawyer doesn't hurt.

"The most important aspect of a patent case is a good story," says the soft-spoken litigator, "but there needs to be more. Other key elements are substantial damages to recover, a good client or inventor to put on the stand, multiple patents to assert, and multiple defendants."

Schutz gravitates toward contingency work when partners at few established firms would even think about it. He is aware of the risks, as are his partners, but they prefer the risk/reward of selectively putting their skills and bank accounts where their beliefs are. "Our firm has a culture that supports it," he says. In 2003, *American Lawyer* named the litigation department at Robins Kaplan Miller & Ciresi, of which he is chair, IP Litigation Department of the Year.

Other major intellectual property cases won by his department include, *Eolas Technologies, Inc. and The Regents of the University of California v. Microsoft Corporation* ($565 million); *Pitney Bowes Inc. v. Hewlett-Packard Co.* ($400 million); *Intergraph v. Dell Inc.,*

Gateway Inc., and Hewlett-Packard Co. (total settlements $396 million); *Unocal Corp. v. ARCO, Chevron, Exxon, Mobil, Shell and Texaco* (total judgment $91 million).

Schutz is married to his high school sweetheart, Janet, and has three children, one of whom is a cadet at the U.S. Military Academy at West Point. He enjoys hunting, mostly pheasant and some deer, in South Dakota. When the weather permits it, he drives a Mercedes SL 500 convertible, otherwise it is a Cadillac Escalade, but he is not very particular what he travels in.

The chapter that follows, "It Takes More Than Being Right to Win a Patent Dispute," deals with the persistent focus that attorneys, patentees, and investors must have when it comes to succeeding with complex disputes. Almost all of Schutz's cases today are taken on contingency, and he has won awards or settlements for clients from the likes of Canon, Fuji, and Sony.

Patent litigation is expensive and risky—not for the faint of heart. It often resembles trench warfare, with well-financed armies facing each other across a battlefield littered with landmines and bodies.

Just as in actual hand-to-hand combat, no patent litigation battle plan survives first contact with the enemy. Although victory can never be assured, it is necessary to be as prepared as possible before the first shot is fired. Equally important is that no one should start a patent lawsuit without fully understanding the risks, rewards, and hazards. Many people at first glance will understand the rewards of patent litigation: money damages, an injunction that can suspend sales of an infringing product, and the elimination of a competitor. Those same people will also understand at least some of the risks: loss of the patent through an invalidity finding, the risk of counterassertion, and lots of money in attorneys' fees and expenses. Few people fully appreciate the hazards along the way, and there are many, for both the victor and the vanquished. And fewer people still appreciate what it takes to make a winnable patent infringement case.

A strong patent alone does not make a winnable patent case. Many factors go into making a winnable case. A strong patent is just the start.

KNOW EVERYTHING THAT CAN BE KNOWN

The key to victory in a patent case is no different from the key to victory in any other case—the facts. Facts win cases. Patent law is complicated, and there are many traps for the unwary. But a mastery of patent law with all of its intricacies will not yield a victory if the facts are bad. Although it is impossible to know all of the facts at the beginning of a case, there is no excuse for not knowing everything that can be known. *Due diligence often is the difference between an expensive quagmire resulting in defeat and a victory.*

Anyone undertaking patent litigation needs to be in it for the long haul. Many are not. Every case should be pursued as if it will go to trial. The right law firm in this endeavor is essential. Although many law firms try patent cases, there are not as many such firms as you might think. Many firms aggressively (and expensively) litigate up to the courthouse steps and then settle. Although many cases do settle, and this technique sometimes works, maximum settlement value can only be achieved with the absolutely credible threat of having a judge and jury decide the case. Every action taken in pursuing the case needs to be with an eye toward how a judge and jury will perceive the case. This cannot be left to chance.

The key question every patent holder must ask before filing suit is, "Why should the jury vote for us?" Juries may struggle with the intricacies of patent law and the technology of the patent, but at the end of the day, they want to do the right thing and will rely on their sense of right and wrong in reaching a decision. Jurors are people, and people are preconditioned from an early age to make decisions in this manner. From children's stories to television shows to movies, a recurring theme is the battle between good and evil [see Chapter 4, "On Patent Trolls and Other Myths"]. Although not every patent case can be presented in such a stark contrast between good and evil, it is essential that the jury view you as the party wearing the white hat. If at all possible, we like to turn every patent case into a copying case. Juries may struggle with the concept of patent infringement, but they do not struggle at all with the concept of unauthorized copying. They know that copying is bad.

JURIES LOVE A GOOD STORY

At the outset, it is important to characterize the patents to be enforced. If the patent or patents are held by an operating company, they can be put into one of three categories: (1) core patents, (2) peripheral patents, and (3) orphan patents. The characterization of the patents to be enforced will drive the strategic decisions in the litigation. If the patent or patents to be enforced are not held by an operating company but have been acquired by a company solely for the purpose of licensing, then there are several unique challenges to enforcement.

Core patents are those patents being practiced by the patent holder (i.e., those patents that have resulted in commercial embodiments). These patents give the patent holder a competitive advantage in the marketplace and prevent others from entering the market—but only if they are enforced. If someone is infringing a core patent, and the patent holder decides to sue, it is normally with the view toward driving the competitor from the market by obtaining an injunction or settling under terms that allow the competitor to license the patent but at a royalty rate that places them at a commercial disadvantage.

Core patents enjoy an advantage inside the courtroom. Juries love a good story, and core patents usually come with a good story because there is a real product or service behind the patent. Every core patent has its genesis in a need or a problem. Every core patent is a solution. Every core patent has resulted in a product or service that has made life safer or more enjoyable. Telling the story goes a long way toward winning the case.

Peripheral patents are those patents that relate to the business of the patent holder but are not essential. They may be improvement patents or patents not associated with a highly valuable product. These patents will usually not act as barriers to entry of a competitor in the marketplace and can be enforced with the view that a license is an acceptable outcome. Peripheral patents enjoy many of the same advantages inside the courtroom as core patents.

Orphan patents are those patents held by the patent holder that are not associated with any commercial product manufactured by the patent holder. They may be the result of R&D efforts that did not result in a commercial embodiment or that at one time were connected with a commercial product that has been abandoned. The primary value of these patents is in generating revenue. They do not serve as a barrier to entry of a competitor. Some orphan patents may enjoy many of the same advantages inside the courtroom as core patents. In fact, some orphan patents may enjoy greater benefits if the patent holder at one time sold a product covered by the patent but no longer does so. Because the market has been taken over by an infringer, there is a great story to tell.

Patents held by licensing IP companies present unique challenges for enforcement. Often, licensing companies have acquired the patents solely for purposes of licensing or suing to generate revenue. If the patent owner is not in a business relationship with the patent inventor, there is often a less compelling story to tell inside the courtroom.

IDENTIFYING STRONG PATENTS

Strong patents have certain identifiable characteristics. Rule number one: more is better. Asserting multiple patents is almost without exception preferable to asserting only one patent. The rationale is simple: the more arrows in your quiver, the more likely you are to succeed in hitting your target.

The key objective characteristic of a strong patent is clarity. The invention of a patent is legally defined by the claims at the end of the patent specification. Claims are often written in legal language that has only a slight resemblance to English. The best patents are those with clear understandable claims. The prevailing mood of the courts today is to construe patent claims narrowly. This means that the strongest patents are those where the claim terms can be easily mapped to an infringing product (i.e., they "read" on the product). It is also important that the specification of the patent (the part that describes the invention in detail) actually describes the product or method accused of infringement. In other words, if a reasonably intelligent and well-educated juror read the patent specification and then looked at the accused product or method, he or she should easily come to the conclusion that the specification and the accused product or method are the same.

Another objective characteristic of a strong patent is that it tells a story. There is an enormous disparity in the quality of patents, resulting from poor draftsmanship, lack of foresight, lack of time or resources in prosecuting the patent, or some combination of these. Strong patents have a clear specification with a sufficient amount of detail about the background of the technology, the state of the art, the need for the invention, the advantages of the invention, and a detailed description of the invention. In addition, the specification needs to be written in a nonlimiting manner. Defendants will seize on any opportunity to point to statements in the specification as support for limiting the scope of the patent. A well-written patent specification will contain statements that the details are not exhaustive but are just examples and that one of skill in the art would appreciate additional advantages and aspects of the invention.

Another important characteristic is that the patent not carry any baggage. In the process of applying for a patent, the inventor (or usually his or her attorney) and the patent examiner exchange correspondence regarding whether the patent office should grant the inventor a patent. This is part of what is called *patent prosecution*. Typically, the United States Patent and Trademark Office (USPTO) will initially reject a patent application, usually on the basis that there is some prior art that is the same or close to the invention. The inventor then needs to convince the patent examiner that he or she is entitled to a patent. During this exchange, the inventor can make statements that a defendant will point to as limiting the scope of the patent. Strong patents are those where the inventor has not said anything limiting about his or her invention to the USPTO that can be brought up during a dispute.

In addition to having multiple patents to assert, it is a significant advantage if there is a continuation application pending. A continuation patent application is based on the original patent and is entitled to the same filing or priority date. Having a continuation patent application on file allows the patent holder to do two important things: (1) the patent holder can draft new patent claims with the benefit of knowledge of the infringing product or method, and (2) the patent holder can send to the USPTO any prior art that the alleged infringer claims would invalidate the patent.

Good Guys and Bad Guys

At the end of the day, juries want to do the right thing. They want to reward the good guys and punish the bad guys. If at all possible, we like to turn patent cases into a morality play. This requires a client with whom the jury can identify. The best client is one who has been wronged. Sometimes individual inventors are the best clients and sometimes they are not. Sometimes the best client can be an international corporate behemoth. The ideal client is either a lone sympathetic inventor or a company with patents by a lone sympathetic inventor.

Another factor that makes for a great client is one who is practicing the patent (i.e., the patent is a core patent). At trial, the case needs to be presented through witnesses. Ideally, the patent holder, if a corporate entity, would like to have the inventor or inventors testify. In today's corporate environment, however, the inventor may be long departed by the time a patent issues and the case goes to trial. This is the perfect illustration of why a strong patent alone is not enough to win a patent case. Someone needs to get on the witness stand and tell the story. If the inventor is not available, then you have a challenge; you need an inventor substitute. This can be someone who worked with the inventor or the hired technical expert witness.

Before filing suit, it is imperative to know who is going to tell the story. Clients who may not be particularly sympathetic are those who own patents they are not practicing. This includes not only operating companies but also companies whose primary function is acquiring and enforcing patents. Many such companies have arisen in the last decade, and there is currently a vigorous debate about their activities (see chapter seven). Most of the complaints about these licensing companies come from large corporate entities who complain that they are victims. These companies have labeled patent licensing companies, among other things, as "patent trolls." It is not the purpose of this chapter to debate this issue. Rather, if the patent holder is someone who is not practicing the patent, then it is important to anticipate an attack from the defendant that this makes the patent holder appear less worthy of relief in court.

The flip side of the client coin is the defendant. The ideal defendant (from a plaintiff's perspective) is a competitor of the patent holder, preferably a much larger competitor. This situation sets up the classic David vs. Goliath struggle in which juries almost invariably favor David. Having a strong patent and a winnable case does not clearly lead to the conclusion that you should file a lawsuit. Even winnable cases can be lost. The next step in the analysis requires a clear understanding of the risks and rewards.

PATENT DISPUTES: MEASURING RISK AND REWARD

The rewards of patent litigation can be significant. The rewards can include monetary damages in the form of lost profits or a reasonable royalty and also an injunction (preventing the sale of a product), which can be worth far more than monetary damages. The size of jury verdicts in patent cases in recent years has skyrocketed. Recent jury verdicts have also increased the size of settlements. There are numerous risks involved in patent litigation. As mentioned, patent litigation is expensive. Every two years, the American Intellectual Property Law Association (AIPLA) conducts an economic survey. According to the AIPLA, the cost of a patent case through trial in California, where more than $25 million is at stake, is approximately $5 million. It is not unusual, however, for patent cases to cost substantially more than this figure. This is money that may be better spent on other endeavors.

Another risk is that you will be countersued for patent infringement. When a patent holder sues a competitor, it is highly likely that the competitor, too, will have patents. If so, it will be highly advantageous to the defendant to counter sue for patent infringement. Or worse, if the defendant has several patents that it thinks the plaintiff is infringing, it may counter sue for patent infringement and also file an affirmative case for patent infringement in a more favorable jurisdiction. Then, instead of having a simple patent infringement case, the patent holder will find itself charged with patent infringement in the same suit and also charged with patent infringement in another jurisdiction.

Yet another risk of patent litigation is that the patents are found to be invalid or unenforceable. For the patent holder to win, everything must go right. The defendant, however, only has to prevail on one of many available defenses.

WAYS TO "KILL" A PATENT

There are many ways to kill a patent. A nonexhaustive list follows.

- Anticipation
- Obviousness
- On sale bar
- Best mode
- Enablement
- Lack of written description
- Indefiniteness
- Improper inventorship
- Inequitable conduct
- Laches
- Estoppel

If you are a large company, enforcing your patents can result in another type of risk—an anti-trust counterclaim. Patent litigation is not only expensive for both sides but also highly distracting to any operating company. Patent litigation requires a lot of support from the clients. Each side will demand the production of large amounts of information (often, which comes out in cost discovery), much of it highly sensitive. Gathering this information, in the form of documents, computer data, and e-mails, is extremely time consuming and disruptive to accomplishing day-to-day work. In addition, many employees will probably be deposed. Yet another hazard is that the patent will be put into reexamination with the USPTO. (Anyone can request a reexamination, and a USPTO director can request one, as well.)

HEDGING THE RISK

One way to reduce the financial risk of patent litigation is to retain a law firm to take the case on a contingent-fee basis. Is it a good thing that some law firms are willing to take patent cases on a contingent-fee basis? Clearly, the answer is yes. Because patent litigation is so expensive, if firms were unwilling to take on such cases, individual inventors and small companies would be left without any recourse when faced with a well-funded infringer. Many start-up companies would be stillborn because a larger competitor took their patented technology. Law firms that are willing to undertake contingent-fee patent litigation level the playing field.

Although more firms are willing to undertake contingent-fee patent litigation today than previously, the numbers are still small. The primary reason for this is that most law firms are risk averse. Most firms are content to bill their attorneys' hours at market rates, and provide no contingent-fee litigation of any kind. Even those firms that have a history of contingent-fee litigation are often reluctant to undertake contingent-fee patent litigation because the risk of the unknown is far greater than in other types of contingent-fee litigation. Those firms that have the most success at contingent-fee patent litigation have three traits in common: (1) they have a history of taking cases of different kinds on a contingent-fee basis; (2) they have a supportive firm culture; and (3) they are well capitalized.

When a company or an individual inventor asks my firm to take a patent case on a contingent-fee basis, we are in effect acting as merchant bankers, investing our own capital. As such, we are extremely selective in deciding which cases to take. Many factors go into a litigation risk-reward analysis, and they will vary somewhat depending on the circumstances. A well-financed patent holder, often a large corporation, will approach this analysis from a different perspective than will a law firm analyzing whether to take the case on a contingent-fee basis. The large corporation may believe, for example, that it is necessary to send a message to potential patent asserters who believe they are easy prey that patent assertions will be stopped, not settled, no matter what the cost.

BALANCING RISK AND REWARD

Some of the factors that should be included in the risk-reward analysis include:

- The business objective
- Number of patents to be asserted
- Claim construction issues
- The strength of the infringement case
- Amount of potential damages
- Strength of the validity case
- Nature of the plaintiff (i.e., whether the plaintiff is the inventor, a company practicing the patents, or a licensing organization)
- Status of the inventors (i.e., are they available to testify, employed by the patent owner, etc.)
- Nature of the defendant(s)
- Relationship between the patent holder and the defendant(s)

(continues)

BALANCING RISK AND REWARD (CONTINUED)

- Number of potential defendants
- Resources of the potential defendants
- Whether there are continuation applications pending
- Lost opportunity costs

When Considering Contingency

- Must have a culture that encourages intelligent risk taking
- Must have a good relationship with your partners
- History and experience with contingent-fee litigation
- Must have a good relationship with your bankers or a lot of money in the bank
- One-off cases can be dangerous to your firm
- Partner compensation structure
- Must know how to compensate partners who might not produce any income for several years

He called it The Sleet's crow's-nest, *in honor of himself; he being the original inventor and patentee, and free from ridiculous false delicacy, and holding that if we call our own children after our own names (we fathers being the original inventors and patentees), so likely should we denominate after ourselves any other apparatus that we might beget.*

—Herman Melville, 1851

CHAPTER 10

Managing Innovation Assets as Business Assets

BY JOE BEYERS

Profile: Master Scout

Joe Beyers once closed 12 patent licensing transactions with Intel in a single day. Normally, it takes anywhere from several months to two years to negotiate a patent license. Every deal that affects intellectual property at Hewlett-Packard crosses his desk. Last year, 2,500 did, and he made changes, he says, that tangibly improved 1,000 of them.

Beyers is part of a new breed of in-house intellectual property strategist, the CIPO, or chief IP officer, who are one part technologist, one part legal expert, and two parts

Scout Master, Joe Beyers (center), with Eagle Scout sons Jeff (left), and Jason.

deal maker. He attributes his ability to get difficult IP agreements completed to his diverse business and technology background and his tenacity. That HP has empowered him with the decision-making authority for its portfolio of more than 18,000 active U.S. and 7,000 foreign patents also helps. For 2004, HP was second only to IBM among U.S. company patent recipients. Its 2002 merger with Compaq, which had previously acquired Digital Equipment, has made HP a formidable IP force by increasing the size and quality of its portfolios of patents, trademarks, copyright, and trade secrets.

"Beyers wields a mighty carrot to persuade HP's various business divisions to work with him in licensing activities," writes IP journalist Victoria Slind-Flor about HP's newly centralized IP function. "There is something in it for every division."

Beyers has the credentials for his job as Vice President for IP Strategy. After more than 27 years with HP, he knows the company inside and out. Most recently, he served as head of strategy and business development for the Computer Systems Business. He also was responsible for driving key strategies and initiatives across HP's $30 billion Computer Organization. This included HP's Internet, networking, and software strategies. He also initiated and managed several key HP external relationships, including those with Microsoft, Netscape, Cisco, and Intel.

An electrical engineer by training, Beyers started his career in research and helped develop the operating system for one of HP's early computers. After that, he was asked to head the company's Integrated Circuit Design Technology Center.

As a rookie researcher, he invented a way of accessing a second computer program while the first program was still running on the same computer. This might sound pretty rudimentary today, but the process was way ahead of its time. Unfortunately, in terms of patent management, HP was not. Beyers was told the company does not enforce patents, and that was that. But he did not forget the wasted opportunity. He went on to head HP's software business and to serve as a key player in the company's M&A activities. If it appears that Beyers, 53, is something of a Boy Scout, ready to make things right, it's because he *is*.

An adult leader and Scout Master for 14 years, Beyers also serves as a youth coach for numerous basketball, baseball, and volleyball teams. To prepare for the physical and mental rigors of negotiation, he trains, bootcamp style, for at least an hour daily starting at 6:00 A.M. He logs at least 100 push-ups, does weight training, and runs several miles. When he ran the Boston Marathon in 1981, 18 months after disc surgery, he finished in the top 10%. His training regimen peaked at 100 miles per week.

It is the spirit of preparedness with which Beyers wants to imbue HP's IP function. He has quadrupled licensing revenues to $200 million in less than 24 months. That's on a P&L level, which does not recognize future royalties until they are paid. Beyers meets biweekly with HP CEO Mark Hurd to discuss opportunities as well as defensive tactics. He is the only IP strategist with dotted-line reporting and direct access to senior management. He also presents quarterly to the Technology Committee of the firm's board of directors, something previously unheard of for an IP manager.

"Financial objectives are not as difficult to explain as strategic ones," says Beyers, who at any one time has about 150 licensing transactions in progress. "It's easier for royalty income to speak for itself. But strategic accomplishments are more qualitative and require context to get your arms around. I enjoy talking about IP to business people. I find them more than willing to listen."

In his chapter, "Managing Innovation Assets as Business Assets," Beyers is adamant about the destruction wrought by patent trolls. The problem, in his view, is that trolls do not make anything themselves, so they have an unfair advantage attacking a company that develops, markets, and sells products. They have little downside. Companies often panic and pay predatory patent asserters to prevent a suit from proceeding, even if they have no case.

In today's competitive business environment, operating companies need to develop products and services that provide unique differentiating value. Businesses also need to defend against potential threats to their well-being. Innovation is essential in order to maintain a competitive advantage. Without it, most companies are doomed.

However, the investment required to create meaningful differentiation—billions of dollars annually for some large technology-based companies—is not sustainable if a business does not understand and receive its full fair value for the investment in innovation. Value comes first from the sale of its products and services, but also through the licensing of its intellectual property to other companies, sometimes even competitors. Licensing IP can be achieved in two ways: either (1) by encouraging new use of this IP by other companies for an appropriate fee (so-called carrot licensing) or (2) by obtaining fair compensation from other companies for its unauthorized use (stick licensing).

Either way, it is a strategic imperative to properly protect the company's IP and to maximize its overall return on its investment in innovation. Failure to do so is a failure of the management team and the board to execute their fiduciary responsibilities to the company's shareholders.

Within this context, a significant transformation of the perception of intellectual property is occurring, particularly with regard to patents. IP rights management is no longer considered an interesting side project of the R&D and legal departments. Instead, it is being regarded as a critical company asset, a core competency to be used (1) for creating a competitive advantage, (2) for IP defensive purposes, and (3) as a vehicle for alternative value generation. CEOs and Boards of Directors have begun to appoint business executives to manage and drive a comprehensive, companywide intellectual property strategy. In some cases, the heads of these functions are referred to as the company's Chief IP Officer (CIPO). Although this term is not universally accepted, it does recognize the strategic importance of IP to companies today.

Senior management oversight typically plays a key role in prioritizing significant company investments, and patents should be no different. Strategies for improved IP protection and defense, and strategies for enhanced monetization of IP, are so important they must come from the top level. A business-led IP licensing program is one that is run by business entrepreneurs who drive IP transactions that fully utilize the assets and market position of the company to its advantage. It is a no-holds-barred engagement that involves the use of innovative business concepts to maximize the overall value obtained in an IP transaction. The first of these groups began to appear in the technology industry in the 1990s. Early pioneers include IBM, Texas Instruments, Lucent, and more recently, HP and Microsoft.

LEGAL VS. BUSINESS-LED IP PERSPECTIVES

Traditionally, companies have tapped their legal department to lead the effort to obtain external value from their IP portfolio (Figure 10.1). This has given way to a growing trend to place this responsibility with a business-driven organization that works in close collaboration with the legal function and senior management. This structure enables companies to implement a significantly more effective IP licensing program —more effective in both the amount and timing of the value received.

Successful execution of an innovative IP licensing program requires a significant amount of business savvy and a true entrepreneurial spirit that encourages out-of-the-box strategies that are lacking at most large companies. A company must be willing to take an appropriate level of risk to do things that have not been done in the company's traditional business model and that will exact a significant return. The factors to consider in a diverse licensing strategy transcend the basic elements of the IP to be licensed. These include purchase commitments, marketing and resell agreements, joint technology development, asset or business

FIGURE 10.1   LEGAL VS. BUSINESS-LED
IP LICENSING

Legal-Led	Business-Led
• Precise	• Entrepreneurial
• Methodical	• Innovative
• Risk Adverse	• Risk Tolerant
• Passive	• Proactive
• IP for Defense	• IP for Offense

sales, IP assertion rights, and executive/relationship leverage. In one such situation, a company was approached to request a license to a few patents for $500,000. The final deal was concluded for $50 million. The transaction included a license to a set of patents, the transfer of ownership of a few patents, a license with modification rights to some software technology, a consulting agreement to enhance this software, assertion rights to some additional patents, and a bilateral set of product and service purchase commitments. The more complex, innovative transaction resulted in a 100-fold increase in realized value.

Although there are exceptions to any generalization, a typical legal environment is often one of precision, structure, and adversity to trouble. By contrast, an entrepreneurial business fosters a more risk-tolerant mentality. Enforcing rights, for example, often carries the threat of counterassertion. There must be close collaboration between the IP business team and the legal function to ensure that the true risks are well understood.

The first step in defining an effective method of using a company's IP assets through licensing is to define the intended scope of the effort. IP can exist in many forms, but the four most common elements of an IP licensing process are patents, copyrights, trademarks, and trade secrets. Each of these assets has different licensing dynamics, but combining all of these in an integrated licensing program frequently lead to better results. For example:

- For a technology that has patents plus trade secrets, the patents can be used to better ensure that if the trade secret information is reverse-engineered, a patent enforcement opportunity still exists.

- A standards-based trademark license can require a specific implementation for which one has patents that reads on this design to better ensure that other companies won't attempt to implement the standard in a way that circumvents the need for a patent license.

- If a technology license requires both a trademark license and a patent license, the trademark is still enforceable even against companies that may have existing broad patent cross-licenses that cover this specific technology domain.

ELEMENTS OF A BUSINESS-LED IP MODEL

An effective business-led IP licensing model has several basic attributes (Figure 10.2), that differ from one that relies on patents as the only company assets.

- **IP is viewed as a corporate asset.** As such, no individual business manager should be allowed to unilaterally encumber this

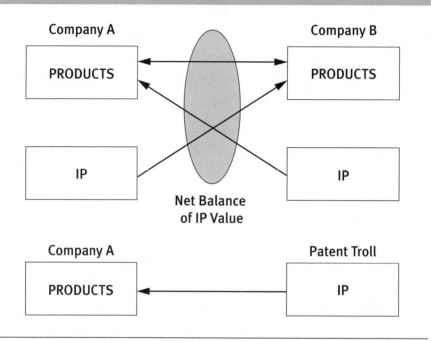

FIGURE 10.2   OPERATING COMPANIES VS.
IP HOLDING COMPANIES

Less to Lose. IP holding companies that do not produce products have less to lose in patent disputes than operating companies that are heavily invested in R&D, sales costs, and human resources.

asset. It is all too easy for a business manager, who is under pressure to meet his or her quarterly sales results, to materially impact a strategic intangible asset if it helps with the short-term bottom line. It is also difficult for any one business to fully account for the cross-company implications of an IP portfolio in, say, a company-to-company IP balance of trade dispute (i.e., a broad patent cross-license with a net balancing payment).

- **The IP licensing program has a high degree of scrutiny and visibility with the CEO and the Board of Directors.** IP actions can have significant implications on the strategic direction of a company—even those that may originally seem to be trivial transactions. These transactions also often involve trade-offs across businesses. Alignment of the IP actions with the company's strategy and top executive support for high-impact and sometimes controversial IP actions is critical for the effective execution of the licensing program.

- **The financial model for the IP licensing function provides the right incentives for a high degree of collaboration with the business units.** Although every executive likes to run his or her own business with separate financial accountability and visibility, running an IP licensing function as a separate full P&L is fraught with problems. It creates an endemic competitive situation with the business units. A far better approach is to centralize IP operations and have the licensing revenue flow back into the appropriate business units. One variation can be to have the licensing function retain a small fixed percentage of the revenue to fund its operation. Overall, this provides the best method of inducing the business units to provide help and support in a licensing action. It also enables the IP licensing function to scope and rationalize the size of its function based on delivering results for the company.

- **Clear roles and responsibilities are defined, and the IP licensing function has sufficient decision-making authority to enable rapid execution.** Any licensing action that could potentially affect an operating business unit needs to be evaluated to ensure that the best company decision is made. Situations will inevitably arise where the objectives of a particular business unit will conflict with an IP licensing action. In this case, a clear and effective escalation or dispute resolution process needs to be established to resolve these issues quickly and with a minimum of internal collateral damage. Failure to have dispute resolution decision-making authority in place will lead to protracted licensing delays and a schism between the IP licensing function and the business units.

- **The IP program is staffed with skilled and experienced specialists.** IP licensing is a difficult, complex, and sometimes risky endeavor. It is not a process that should be driven by novices, and it requires a great amount of creativity and tenacity. Patent licensing is often viewed as one of the most difficult negotiations. It is a process in which one is asking someone for money for something they cannot see or touch or for the rights to an invention that the other party may already have been practicing for years. A patent license is something that no one wants but everyone needs. It also has the risk that in attempting to *receive* $1 million in value in a transaction, one could end up *paying* $10 million to $100 million instead or have a product line shut down as a result of unleashing a counterattack from the target that was originally approached. A company's executive management or that of an affected business unit is usually unforgiving when and if these situations arise. The old adage, "It takes 100 'atta-boys' to undue one 'ah-sh—'," definitely applies to this business activity. For this reason, the people engaged in licensing need to have a real passion for their work. Otherwise, the pressure and frustration of the licensing process will wear them down and they will become ineffective.

- **Sufficient infrastructure exists to enable effective execution.** It is extremely important that a good set of IP databases and analysis tools are available to the IP licensing program. In any licensing action, the licensing agents need to have a thorough understanding of both the company's IP as well as that of the potential licensee. The Sun Tsu principles of knowing yourself and knowing your enemies are critical. Failure to have this analysis capability and the knowledge that comes from it can result in a licensing action taking a surprising destructive turn or a missed opportunity to bring the full leverage of a company's assets to the table in the negotiations.

How Patent Trolls Affect Profits

The previous sections presented a model of how an operating company can maximize the value that it receives from its intellectual assets. This section describes the emergence of a new kind of business model working at odds with operating companies to undermine their hard-earned gains. Participants in this newly emerged model are frequently referred to as patent "trolls."

There is no industry standard definition of a patent troll. One proposed definition is of a company or business whose primary objective is to buy patents and assert them or, effectively, to use them to sue other companies to realize a return on the purchase and assertion costs. A patent troll is not necessarily unethical in its actions. However, it has the ability to extract an unfair value for its patents from operating companies, thanks to the current nature of the patent laws and judicial system. This ability to extract unfair value by exploiting the system is the root of the problem with the patent troll model, and it poses a significant threat to companies that practice patents, especially to those that are heavily invested in R&D.

An inventor deserves the right to obtain a fair value for his or her inventions—either directly or through a broker or agent. Individual inventors or companies who are not providing products have been asserting patents against operating companies for years. The emergence of the recent patent troll phenomenon occurred in the aftermath of the dot-com bust. During its peak, many companies created some interesting inventions, using the capital obtained through inflated market valuations. As the bubble burst, many companies decomposed into an empty office building and a set of patent assets. These rights were often auctioned, traded, and brokered. Speculative investment money materialized from venture capital funds, individual investors, and in some cases even Global 1,000 operating companies to buy these patents for the purpose of getting a return via a patent assertion. Thus, the patent troll model emerged.

Several patent troll businesses have been formed, some with many hundreds of millions of dollars in a war chest to fund patent acquisitions and assertions. A typical operating process for such an entity is to quietly acquire patents—sometimes through an agent so that the acquirer is disguised—and wait until a significant portfolio is amassed before it launches an attack.

As the supply of the dot-com patent assets is being consumed by the marketplace, the patent trolls are now looking to at least two different sources of patent assets. The first is by acquiring small or near-dead companies that have strong IP portfolios. As reported by *Forbes,* the $200 million private equity fund backed by Ross Perot was created for such a purpose. A second channel is to approach operating companies and convince (or coerce) them to sell some of their patent portfolios. This is done through either an outright acquisition, a purchase with a contingency fee structure whereby the original company gets a percentage of the proceeds realized by the patent troll in the enforcement of the patents, or through coercion by threatening the company with other patents in order to get ownership of these patents. The net result is that the patent trolls are getting access to a richer set of potentially enforceable patents and often are doing so in more covert and less competitive transactions.

THE NATURE OF THE UNFAIR VALUE THAT PATENT TROLLS CAN REALIZE

It can always be argued that "value" is a subjective and ambiguous term. On the one hand, value is whatever a willing buyer will pay for something. On the other hand, a myriad of analytical models try to precisely quantify patent value. In reality, real value, in the context of patent valuation, is a mixture of both perspectives. Analytical models can indicate what the value should be in a hypothetical, ideal environment. What one is actually willing to pay for an IP asset ultimately comes down to an assessment of what leverage one party has over the other party relative to the ideal valuation model. It has more to do with risk analysis than market value. Given this perspective, a critical element in executing a patent transaction for a "fair" value is to first make sure that the tools or weapons used in the engagement are fair. In a prize fight, it is not fair if one fighter has an iron bar in his glove and the other one doesn't. Given the current state of the patent laws and their implementation in the judicial system, an attack on an operating company by a patent troll has many striking similarities to such a prize fight.

Three primary factors create an imbalance between patent trolls and operating companies in the quest to assign fair value to IP: (1) uncertainty in the litigation process, (2) injunctive relief, and (3) patent reexamination.

There is an extreme amount of uncertainty in a patent litigation process. In a jury trial, juries typically do not fully understand the technical nature of infringement and patent invalidity, yet they are asked to decide which ones of many expert witnesses with opposing positions are correct. In mock trials of these cases, it is quite common to have two mock juries hear identical testimony and have each jury reach unanimous yet opposing verdicts. With this backdrop, an operating company being sued by a patent troll is faced with a difficult scenario with an extremely high degree of uncertainty as to the eventual outcome of a jury trial.

A second major factor in the imbalance between a patent troll and an operating company is that a troll is often able to obtain an injunction to stop the other company's product shipments if in the first round of litigation the patents are found to be valid and infringed, even though the patent troll does not ship products itself. The original intent of the injunction concept was to provide a company with recourse if continued shipments of a product was causing the holder of the IP "irreparable harm." For example, if company A is shipping printers that infringe the patents of printer company B, then company B is suffering "irreparable harm" if company A continues shipping infringing products. A patent troll suffers no such harm if the operating company continues to ship products during the dispute. Given the uncertainty of the litigation outcomes described earlier, this creates a draconian downside scenario for the operating company. Even when the likelihood of a ruling against an operating company is low, the impact of its potential occurrence is often too severe to let the case go to court. As a result, an operating company will often provide a payout to a troll that is higher than what should have been viewed as a fair value for a license on the troll's patents.

A third flaw in the patent process that tips the balance of patent valuation in a troll's favor is the issue of patent reexamination. The U.S. Patent and Trademark Office is doing its best to manage a deluge of patent applications, but it is understaffed and overworked. As a result, frequently questionable patents are issued when they never should have seen the light of day. In a patent assertion, it is difficult to force a patent reexamination. In most cases, the only viable recourse for determining invalidity is through the litigation process. Here again, the uncertainty factor in litigation often results in an operating company paying off a patent troll for a patent that it is convinced is invalid. Furthermore, in some Federal Court jurisdictions, patents are almost never ruled to be invalid. The rules for patent reexamination need to be liberalized. An adequately staffed, well-funded patent office —not a judge or a jury—should be the prime avenue for further determining patent validity.

A predecessor to the word "patent troll" was the phrase "patent terrorist," which was used by Intel until it was ultimately sued for slander for labeling another company with this term [see chapters five and seven]. The word "troll" was substituted to represent the concept of a toll taker who extracts a fee for crossing a bridge, probably as a variant of the Scandinavian fairy tale troll. Provided that the troll does own the bridge, the charge of a fee for the right to cross the bridge is a legitimate business process. However, in the fairy tales, such as in the *Three Billy Goats Gruff,* the troll is a hideous character who scares people into paying far more than a reasonable rate for crossing the bridge—sometimes with their lives. It is interesting to note that in both uses of the troll concept—the fairy tale bridge troll and the modern patent troll—the troll extracts an unfair value for its service.

WHAT OPERATING COMPANIES CAN DO TO PROTECT THEMSELVES

There are two key approaches to reduce the risk of operating companies being unfairly attacked by patent trolls. One action is for these companies to attempt to bid for and purchase patents before a patent troll does. This is rarely practical to implement and usually too expensive to execute. For one thing, a patent troll will likely be able to extract a higher value for the assertion of the patents than any one company would save by acquiring them. Most trolls can usually outbid any single company. A second factor is that few, if any, normal operating companies have the dedicated resources to aggressively scan for and execute patent acquisition opportunities of this type. The patent troll has a highly incentivized staff of professionals who are engaged full time to find and acquire these patent assets and evaluate them.

The information technology industries should drive collectively for patent reform to attempt to "declaw" the trolls. The two top priorities are the elimination of the troll's ability to force an injunction on an operating company, particularly while the patents are still being disputed through the courts, and a reformation of the patent reexamination process. Although these actions will not completely eliminate an operating company's risk from the patent trolls, they will at least lead to more even-handed dispute resolution.

The business of intellectual property has significantly changed over the last several years. IP today is a core strategic business asset that needs to be effectively managed and properly utilized. It is also increasingly being used as a weapon against businesses as a result of the emergence of a new business model, the patent troll. Optimizing the effective use and defense of a company's IP assets is an important step toward competitive advantage and shareholder value, and more companies are prepared to take it.

A country without a patent office and good patent laws is just a crab and can't travel any way but sideways and backwards.

—Mark Twain, 1889

CHAPTER 11

Secrets of the Trade: An Inventor Shares His Licensing Know-How

BY RONALD A. KATZ

Profile: An American Original

The next time a call center asks you to "select one for this, two for that, or three for the other thing," think of Ron Katz. He is virtually everywhere. But Katz has received surprisingly little recognition. His detractors, possible infringers and their representatives, paint him as a troll, fishing around for a vulnerable company to sue. In fact, over four decades, Katz has identified, patented, practiced, and licensed dozens of inventions that scores of companies need to do business. If anyone qualifies as an American pioneer on the knowledge frontier, it is Katz, but don't expect to see him on the cover of *Time* magazine anytime soon.

Ron Katz enjoys fly fishing for salmon in British Columbia. He leaves the trolling to others.

The most financially successful inventor in history, Katz has generated patent licensing revenues to date approaching $1 billion on his call center patents and expects to double that figure by 2009. An independent inventor with unique patience and abundant resources, he is a role model to inventors, investors, and managers alike, although few are willing to admit it.

In 1961, Katz, age 24, and partner Robert N. Goldman formed publicly owned Telecredit, Inc., the nation's first real-time credit and check cashing verification service. They were granted a U.S. patent on the invention that underlied the company's products. When Telecredit hit some rough spots, Katz turned to licensing for additional revenue. "This was prior to the Federal Circuit Court of Appeals, and patent owners were having difficulty prevailing in court," says Katz. "Pursuing reasonable settlements by offering fair terms was the only way to go."

Around 1985, Katz saw the potential of combining computers with telephones to achieve new forms of interactive processing. He is named on more than 50 issued U.S. patents covering systems relating to automated call centers, interactive voice response, credit verification, video monitoring, anti-counterfeit, and merchandise verification.

Katz hails from a creative family. His dad, Mickey Katz, was a successful comedian and klezmer musician responsible for ethnic self-parodies such as "How Much is that Pickle in the Window" and "Knish Doctor." He moved the family from Cleveland to Los Angeles when Katz was 8 years old. Older brother, actor Joel Grey, is best known for his award-winning role as the master of ceremonies in both the stage and film versions of *Cabaret*. Grey's daughter, Jennifer, Katz's niece, also a film actor, starred with Patrick Swayze in *Dirty Dancing*.

"He has never studied engineering or computer science," observes Evan I. Schwartz in his profile on Katz in *Juice: The Creative Fuel that Drives Today's World-Class Inventors* (Harvard Business School Press, 2004), "and yet was the first to sketch out a critical set of new information technologies that the world would want and need, an achievement that has put many major corporations on the defensive."

Studying back-office transactions, such as voluminous check and phone call processing, and thinking about ways to improve them are among Katz's interests. He enjoys identifying ways of making businesses more efficient, and he has helped streamline processes or make them more reliable. Companies tend to take these improvements for granted and will pay for them only when they must. Schwartz notes that a visitor [to Katz's small office in Los Angeles] "sees no clutter, no gadgets, no machine tools, and no engineers at graphical workstations."

Katz, now 69, helped change how innovation is understood by regarding information processing as a series of inventions that can be enhanced, protected, and made quantifiably more profitable.

"Companies will consider taking a license when you show them the value," says Katz, who is proud of his record of never having gone to trial, although he has always been prepared to do so, if necessary. "Initial reactions can vary widely, and [companies] often need to be convinced it is in their own best interest to pay. Often, it's easier to get management to agree to pay a reasonable royalty rather than bury their head in the sand and risk a large cash verdict and even an injunction."

Katz emphasizes that independent and large corporate inventors alike must have the goods to succeed: good invention, good patents that read on them, and the resources and resolve to persevere in disputes with infringers. Katz has guest-lectured on negotiations for 12 years at Stanford University's Graduate School of Business. Through Ronald A. Katz Technology Licensing, L.P., and its affiliate, Katz has successfully negotiated more than 150 patent licenses to such companies as IBM; Microsoft; Home Shopping Network; AT&T; MCI; Sprint; Verizon; Sears, Roebuck and Co.; Delta Air Lines; Bank of America; Merck; and Vanguard. He has never had to go to trial.

Although the troll image may be an inaccurate depiction of him, the fishing one is not. Katz likes to get away from it all by salmon fishing in remote areas of British Columbia. He also enjoys spending time with his six grandchildren in Hawaii where, he says, "I can walk on the beach, clear my head, and come up with new ideas."

Despite his successes—or some speculate because of them—a rare *ex parte* (or USPTO Commissioner–requested reexamination of four of his call center patents was initiated in 2005). If successful, it could impact some of Katz's future enforcement efforts. (He has 48 other interactive call-processing patents fully intact.) If not, it is sure to reaffirm the value of his rights and ability to enforce them. Some believe that under intense political pressure, the USPTO is succumbing, preemptively, to companies who fear that it is only a matter of time before they will have to take a Katz license. But this is not stopping Katz. In July 2005, RAKTL filed a patent infringement suit for his call center patents against Citigroup, Morgan Stanley's Discover Financial Services, T-Mobile USA, and Wal-Mart Stores.

In the following chapter, Katz discusses his licensing career and some of the strategies he and his tiny team employ when talking to companies about efficiencies they might otherwise take for granted. It is a window into the workings of an original American thinker and entrepreneur.

The licensing program for the Katz interactive call-processing patent portfolio is one of the most successful in history. With licensing revenues to date approaching the $1 billion mark, it provides a useful lesson for inventors and investors alike. However, experience I gained through participation in several earlier pioneering developments as an entrepreneur, business executive, and inventor played a significant part in the success of the call-processing portfolio. By sharing some of these earlier experiences, I hope other inventors, as well as managers and shareholders, can better understand how I have made a small patent licensing program successful, and that you do not have to be a large company with massive numbers of patents to succeed.

It started with the formation of a company called Telecredit Inc. more than 40 years ago. In 1961, using technology on which we had filed for patent protection, Telecredit operated the first call center dedicated to online, real-time credit authorization. It may well have been the first computerized call center in the United States. In late 1961, we started providing services in our new call center facility, which used an automatic call distributor for receiving and distributing calls, live operators to handle calls from merchants, and multiple buffered input-output stations connected to two back-to-back computers. Operators would take calls from merchants, who would provide the operators with identification information for the customer, who was offering the merchant a check. Typically, the identifying information would be a driver's license. The operator would input the identifying information into the system, and the system would search its database to determine whether the identified person had, for example, passed a bad check, cashed a second payroll check in a given week at another merchant location, or engaged in some other activity that should cause the merchant concern about cashing the check.

Telecredit was praised for having played a major role in reducing bad check crime in the Los Angeles area. Passing bad checks was rampant at this time.[1] During 1962, Telecredit's first full year of operation, the check-forgery rate in L.A. decreased for the first time in several years, and it did so by 8%. Our system was so effective that, during the first few years, it resulted in the arrest of thousands of "bad check passers"

---

[1] Bad check crime was depicted in a 2004 film, *Catch Me If You Can,* starring Leonardo DiCaprio and directed by Steven Spielberg.

in real time—while they were in the process of cashing their checks. In 1963, we developed and distributed what I believe was the world's first bank-check-guarantee card, and we developed a system to control the use of these cards. This was the forerunner of today's "check cards" issued by banks. In 1964, we built and commercialized what I believe was the world's first online, real-time point-of-service (POS) device that accessed a dynamic memory database.

In the 1970s, we licensed the Telecredit patent portfolio on a worldwide basis to a large number of companies, including IBM, NCR, Diebold, and Chubb. In the late 1980s, Equifax bought Telecredit for just under $1 billion.

THE BUSINESS MODEL

What we did with Telecredit, in broad terms, set the pattern for my future efforts: (1) identify new technology, systems, and processes; (2) develop the inventions; (3) patent the inventions; (4) set up a company to practice the inventions; (5) continue to develop new, related inventions that add value by providing the growing market with more technology, systems, and processes that people need or want; and (6) operate the business in a way that leads to commercial success.

Our next effort began in 1983. We developed, patented, and commercialized a system for producing noncounterfeitable labels and cards and tracking these units in commerce. To operate this system, we created a company called Light Signatures, Inc. The system passed a light beam through the label or card that was being protected. (Levi Strauss, the blue jeans manufacturer, was one of the first customers for the system.) The Light Signatures system then encoded a machine-readable number for the unique light pattern read by the device on the label or card. The label could be read by a decoder at a later time to verify its authenticity and trace its use in channels of commerce. The technology was elegant and sufficiently bulletproof that no one was ever able to create a counterfeit Light Signature–encoded label or card that could escape detection by our decoding device—and some very sophisticated people tried to do it.

In 1985, I turned my attention to interactive call handling. I realized this technology could save companies the significant costs associated with running live-agent call centers and handle calls on a massive scale. That same year, I filed my first patent application for the interactive call-processing portfolio dealing with interactive voice-response systems.

In 1988, I entered into a joint venture with American Express to establish a new company to commercialize my interactive call-processing inventions. The joint venture was known as FDR Interactive Technologies. Together we built and programmed a system, the centerpiece of which became the largest and most sophisticated interactive call-processing platform developed to that date. It had 10,000 active incoming lines—to serve a wide variety of leading-edge call-processing applications (Figure 11.1).

In 1989, we implemented our first commercial services, with some of our first clients being the *New York Times,* KABC Radio, and Monday Night Football. Later that year, I sold my interest in the joint venture to American Express, which then sold it to AT&T. Then, while on the road to what I thought was retirement, I agreed to provide consulting services to the newly formed joint venture between AT&T and American Express Information Services Co., which was named Call Interactive. I also continued to invent new call-processing technologies, and the patent portfolio grew increasingly larger over the next few years. During the period from 1987 to 1993, I filed more than 25 patent applications, and during the same time period, more than 20 U.S. patents were granted and issued. From 1989 on, Call Interactive

FIGURE 11.1   THE KATZ INTERACTIVE CALL CENTER PATENT

United States Patent [19]

Katz

[11] Patent Number: **4,792,968**

[45] Date of Patent: **Dec. 20, 1988**

[54] **STATISTICAL ANALYSIS SYSTEM FOR USE WITH PUBLIC COMMUNICATION FACILITY**

[75] Inventor: **Ronald A. Katz,** Los Angeles, Calif.

[73] Assignee: **FDR Interactive Technologies,** New York, N.Y.

[21] Appl. No.: **18,244**

[22] Filed: **Feb. 24, 1987**

Related U.S. Application Data

[63] Continuation-in-part of Ser. No. 753,299, Jul. 10, 1985, abandoned.

[51] Int. Cl.⁴ **H04M 11/06**
[52] U.S. Cl. **379/92;** 379/67
[58] Field of Search 379/91, 67, 92, 110; 235/377, 375

[56]   **References Cited**

U.S. PATENT DOCUMENTS

3,393,272	7/1968	Hanson	379/67
3,934,095	1/1976	Mathews et al.	379/67
4,017,835	4/1977	Randolph	235/379
4,290,141	9/1981	Anderson et al.	455/2
4,320,256	3/1982	Freeman	379/92
4,345,315	8/1982	Cadotte, et al.	364/900
4,355,207	10/1982	Curtin	379/67
4,355,372	10/1982	Johnson et al.	364/900
4,439,636	3/1984	Newkirk et al.	379/91
4,451,700	5/1984	Kempner et al.	379/88
4,489,438	12/1984	Hughes	381/51
4,521,643	6/1985	DuPuis et al.	379/92
4,523,055	6/1985	Hohl et al.	379/89
4,539,435	9/1985	Eckmann	379/93
4,559,415	12/1985	Bernard et al.	379/91
4,566,030	1/1986	Nickerson	358/84
4,578,700	3/1986	Roberts et al.	358/84
4,584,602	4/1986	Nakagawa	358/84
4,587,379	12/1986	Masuda	379/91
4,603,232	7/1986	Kurland et al.	379/92
4,625,276	11/1986	Benton	364/408
4,630,200	12/1986	Ohmae et al.	364/405
4,630,201	12/1986	White	364/408
4,634,809	1/1987	Paulsson et al.	379/91
4,654,482	3/1987	DeAngelis	379/95
4,674,044	6/1987	Kalmus et al.	364/408
4,696,029	9/1987	Cohen	379/92

4,697,282	9/1987	Winter et al.	379/67

FOREIGN PATENT DOCUMENTS

52-17740	2/1977	Japan	379/91

OTHER PUBLICATIONS

"Voice Mail", *Sound & Communications,* vol. 28, No. 2, 4/83, pp. 84–85.
J. Svigals, "Low Cost Point-of-Sale Terminal", IBM Technical Disclosure Bulletin, vol. 25, No. 4, Sep. 1982.
Goran Erikson, et al., "Voice and Data Workstations and Services in the ISDN", 1984.
A. Turbat, "Telepayment and Electronic Money, The Smart Card", 1982.
V. Scott Borison, "Transaction—Telephone Gets the Facts at the Point of Sale", Bell Laboratories Record, vol. 53, No. 9, Oct. 1975.
M. Demeautis et al., "The TV 200, A Transactional Telephone".

Primary Examiner—Robert Lev
Attorney, Agent, or Firm—Nilsson, Robbins, Dalgarn, Berliner, Carson & Wurst

[57]   **ABSTRACT**

For use with a public communication facility C incorporating terminals T1–TN, e.g. a telephone system, a statistical analysis system D interfaces with individual stations where a caller is prompted by voice instructions to provide digital data that is identified for positive association with the caller and is stored for processing. Caller data is confirmed by a look-up table and by a signal-commanded voice generator. Files are created in the analysis system wherein callers are assigned designations which are stored along with statistical and identification data. In one embodiment, callers are identified by calling sequence and assigned designations are provided in the form of an acknowledgment. A break-off circuit enables a caller to terminate the computer interface aborting to a terminal for direct communication with an operator. The stored data is statistically processed and correlated as with established data to isolate a select group or subset of the callers or caller data that can be readily identified and confirmed.

12 Claims, 4 Drawing Sheets

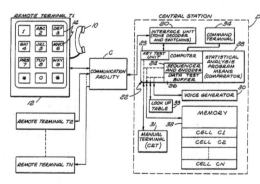

sold its call-processing services to a broad range of packaged-goods companies, TV networks, financial services firms, and other commercial entities, such as the *New York Times*.

During the period from 1991 to 1993, First Data Resources, the American Express unit that operated the call-processing business and held title to the patents, enforced the portfolio twice through litigation. In one case, it succeeded in getting an injunction against the infringer, 900 Million Inc., and the second suit resulted in a large cash settlement, ongoing royalty payments, and a consent judgment acknowledging validity and infringement. In 1992, American Express spun off First Data as a separate company, and with it went the call-processing business and the patents.

In 1994, First Data sold the portfolio of patents back to me, and I established Ronald A. Katz Technology Licensing, L.P., to license the extensive portfolio of patents that we had developed during the prior years. With this transaction, my thoughts of early retirement faded away and a new adventure began.

My first interactive call-processing patent was filed in 1985. As of today, the portfolio includes 52 issued U.S. patents with about 2,500 claims relating to various forms of interactive call processing, and several more pending patent applications. In January 2004, anonymous third parties filed prior-art submissions relating to 16 of the issued patents. In March 2004, the Director of the Patent Office ordered a reexamination of only four of the patents.[2] We have already addressed many of the issues raised in the reexaminations, and we therefore believe

---

[2] "For the losing defendant in a patent infringement case, an *ex parte* [or USPTO ordered] patent reexamination is a shot at redemption," say Maebius, Passino, and Wegner, lawyers at Foley & Lardner. Their June 2004 *Intellectual Property Law & Business* article is subtitled, "The Reexamination Process May be in Need of a Reexamination."

The pillars of this new patent licensing program are and have always been:

- Successful patent prosecution
- Excellent license agreements
- A well-thought-out licensing fee schedule
- An ongoing research program to identify licensing prospects
- A compelling presentation package
- Professional negotiation and licensing capability
- A well-thought-out enforcement plan

that the result of the process will yield reexamined claims that will be even stronger than before.

Agreements and Fee Schedules

Before we began to license, we needed to fashion the first agreement and associated fee schedule. As to the agreement, we considered it important for us to treat it as a work-in-process that would continually need to be refined based on the commercial success of the inventions, the expanding nature of the portfolio, and other developing circumstances. We knew that clarity of terms, provisions to arbitrate disputes, and provisions that allowed for easy accounting were important to the success of the program. Let me note that although our agreements all have an arbitration clause, in the more than 10 years of the program's existence, we have never had to arbitrate any issue with a licensee. I believe that having the arbitration clause in the agreement in and of itself was helpful in ensuring that issues under the license were likely to be resolved through negotiation, rather than requiring some sort of formal procedure for dispute resolution.

Early on, it also became apparent to us that the marketplace really wanted a license to cover use of all of our patents and applications, although we have always been willing to offer a license on individual patents, if requested. We fixed on our principal offering being a "field-of-use" licensing program that allowed a licensee to obtain the necessary rights to all of our patent property in its specific field; for example, we offer licenses in the financial services field of use, the television shopping services field of use, and so on.

We are conscious to offer reasonable, market-sensible license rates. We are able to gauge what is reasonable based on our experience and understanding of the operation of an interactive call-processing business and recognition that one of the primary benefits to a licensee is the cost savings provided by the use of the patented technology. We have elected to raise our rates periodically as the market value of the patents has both increased and become clearer. For example, following the significant AT&T and Verizon settlements, our rates increased, and the value of the patents has become increasingly clearer as companies with their own major patent portfolios and tremendous patent expertise (e.g., IBM, AT&T, and Microsoft) have examined our patents and decided to purchase licenses. Regarding fees, our primary objective is and has been consistency, and we strive to provide consistent pricing to companies in the same fields.

Ongoing Research and Notification Program

We have some wonderfully talented researchers who comb through all sorts of publicly available sources to collect bits and pieces of information. When pieced together, like a jigsaw puzzle, those pieces of information help us identify which companies may be profiting from the use of our patented inventions. We work with our assertion counsel, who helps us assemble that information into a cohesive package that demonstrates the use of our technology. Our assertion counsel will then typically write to the prospective licensee to request a meeting.

Our attorneys prepare for such meetings by creating confidential PowerPoint presentations that take an exemplary claim, element-by-element, and compare it with an operation or method employed by the prospective licensee in its call-processing operations, showing why we

FIGURE 11.2   COMPANIES WITH RAK-LICENSED RIGHTS INCLUDE:

- Advanta Corp.
- Allegheny Power
- American Century
- American Express
- Ameritrade Holding Corp.
- Associated Bank Corp.
- AT&T Corp.
- Automatic Data Processing, Inc.
- Bank of America
- BB&T Corporation
- Cellco Partnership, dba Verizon Wireless
- Certegy Inc.
- Constellation Energy Group, Inc.
- Dell Inc.
- Delta Air Lines, Inc.
- Edward D. Jones & Co., L.P.
- Equifax, Inc.
- Excel Communications
- First Data Corp.
- FirstEnergy Corporation
- First National Bank of Omaha
- First Tennessee National Corporation
- Fiserv, Inc.
- Florida Power & Light
- Hewlett Packard
- Home Shopping Network, Inc.
- Household International, Inc.
- HSBC Bank USA
- IBM
- Illinois Power Company
- KeyCorp
- MCI, Inc.
- Mediacom Communications Corporation
- Mellon Financial Corporation
- Merck & Company
- Metris Companies Inc.
- Microsoft
- MicroVoice Application, Inc.
- Moneygram
- National Grid USA
- Nationwide
- Nicor Inc.
- NSTAR Electric & Gas Corp.
- ONEOK, Inc.
- OppenheimerFunds, Inc.
- People's Bank
- Principal Financial Group, Inc.
- Prudential Financial, Inc.
- Questar
- QVC, Inc.
- Sears, Roebuck and Co.
- Southern California Edison Company
- SouthTrust Bank
- Sprint
- Sunoco, Inc.
- Tampa Electric Company
- The Gallup Organization
- Telecompute Corporation
- Tele-Publishing, Inc.
- T. Rowe Price Associates, Inc.
- The Vanguard Group, Inc.
- Verizon California and its affiliates
- Wachovia Corporation
- Wells Fargo & Company
- Wisconsin Energy Corporation

believe the company is benefiting from the use of our inventions. Our negotiation professionals work with the prospect to finalize a license agreement. We have done this more than 100 times to date (Figure 11.2).

LITIGATION: ALWAYS A LAST RESORT

Our view has always been that we should be able to reach a licensing agreement with any reasonable company that is benefiting from the use of our inventions. Litigation is truly a last resort, and we have initiated litigation only a handful of times in more than a decade. But we also believe that once litigation has commenced, either by us or by someone attacking our patents, we have to act with a resolve whose firmness matches the strength of our belief in our patents.

It is equally important that one has the resources to complete the litigation once it is started. It is important that the infringer recognizes that the individual inventor asserting his or her own patent can afford to continue the litigation. It is my impression that some infringers, or their mega law firms, believe that if they outspend you and delay Judgment Day, the patent owner will yield. In our case, that hasn't worked, primarily because we have both the resolve and the resources to persevere.

We recognize the importance of Markman rulings to interpret the meaning of claim terms. We have had two such rulings—one in the AT&T matter and one in the Verizon matter. Both rulings supported the vast majority of the positions we advocated.

To sum up, here is the box score:

1. The call-processing patent portfolio is one of the most financially successful licensing programs managed by an individual inventor.

2. The patents in the portfolio have been litigated and resulted in a favorable resolution eight times, including the significant AT&T and Verizon settlements.

3. Many of the terms of the patents have been interpreted by the courts in Markman rulings, and those interpretations have generally been favorable.

4. The licensing program continues in full swing. Since the USPTO director–ordered reexaminations, we have completed licensing agreements with 21 additional companies, including several Fortune 500 companies, boosting our licensing revenue totals closer to the $1 billion mark. In addition, many companies are currently negotiating license agreements with us.

Defining Success

I have been asked many times why our licensing program is so successful. I believe the reason is that our patented technology has provided such tremendous value to a wide variety of companies in their marketplace that it has led to phenomenal commercial success. (Many licensees have provided testimonials to support this view.) Also, the technology has provided them with significant shareholder value. There is no substitute for commercially viable inventions coupled with strong patents and the resources and resolve to enforce them.

As more and more companies have found that they had to keep up with consumer demand for customer-service support 24 hours a day, they have often turned to voice-response technology as an effective and efficient alternative to providing hundreds (and in some cases thousands) of live agents to answer calls. The marketplace for sophisticated interactive call processing based on our patented technology has exploded in the last 10 to 15 years and will continue to be integral to many companies' success. It is truly gratifying to have played a part in these advances.

Index